# SHIPWRECKED:
# GROSS MISCONDUCT ON THE HIGH SEAS

by

Deedee Presser

*To the seaman who could never put their anchors away*

# TABLE OF CONTENTS

# INTRODUCTION

When one signs up to work on a cruise ship, in many ways, she is signing away her inalienable rights to be treated with the respect and human decency that our forefathers tried to ensure hundreds of years ago as they penned the United States Constitution- a constitution that, as I came to realize all too quickly, means little to nothing in the baffling world of the luxury cruise industry. The optimism I exhibited as a naïve rookie to what I thought would be this sexy, mysterious, and wanderlust lifestyle as a modern day pirate would quickly be flushed down the toilet of reality. This is not to say that I regret joining the ship—I don't. During my time on the high seas I had the opportunity to make interesting and talented friends from all over the world, hone my French and Spanish skills, learn to play the drums, visit more unbelievably beautiful destinations on a weekly basis than many are able to experience in a lifetime, play sports as part of my job, and, among other things, binge-watch the first five seasons of *House* (which I somehow failed to do during previous spells of unemployment—or, as I like to call it, "funemployment").

Nevertheless, the cruise industry is an industry that many ship outsiders know little about. It is my hope that this exposé enlightens the masses to the underlying discrimination, racism, and altogether crookedness that so pervades the industry, and in doing so, causes changes in a system that are long overdue. The freedom to write something without following conventional methods (i.e. grammatically correct papers with facts checked and sources cited from places other than Wikipedia) seemed all too tempting to pass up as I faced a period of indefinite joblessness— but we'll get to that later.

For anybody who has had the pleasure of partaking on a nautical adventure via one of the world's premier cruise lines, you have experienced firsthand how much work goes into making that one glorious week onboard the most amazing seven days of your life. The extravagant, foreign-labeled cuisine that leaves nobody 100% sure of what they ordered, the entitlement of being waited on 24/7 as if you were a modern day Rose DeWitt Bukater; the lack of judgment that comes from the bartender serving you piña coladas at 10 am; and of course, those delightful little towel creatures that the housekeeping team has ensured will be waiting for you in your room when the day's excitement has come to an end. There's something exotic about being in a different country every morning when you wake up that makes cruising the high seas so much more appealing than taking 15 hour train rides and staying in hostels so cheap that you're forced to make decisions such as whether you want to use the shower that gives off a small jolt every time you touch the metal drain, or the one that somebody confused for a toilet the night before and left a lovely present in for the next patron (or maybe that's just how I travel).

Additionally, cruises offer guests nonstop entertainment, an opportunity to gorge themselves on more food than even Joey Chestnut can fit into his stomach, and the opportunity to abandon even the commonest of sense—an option that several passengers choose to capitalize on with fervent stupidity. Alas, a cruise ship from the viewpoint of a guest can seem like a sort of Shangri-La, but what about the other population on board? The ones who reside in the steerage of the ship for up to nine months at a time without a single day off? I am of course, alluding to the staff and crew of the ship, of which I was a part for approximately 4.5 months. As a former "shipee," embittered by a recent firing and with nothing going for me except a useless master's degree and the ability to fold napkins into roses, I feel obligated to tell the ridiculous story of my brief, yet excruciatingly long time as a member of the sport staff on a Royal Caribbean ship. What follows in the next hundred or so unconventionally organized pages is the remarkable story of one woman's incredible efforts to survive an entire 6.75 month contract in the bowels of the *M.S. Voyager of the Seas.*

# CHAPTER I: WHY THE CRUISE INDUSTRY?

*Lesson I've learned the hard way #16: When interviewers ask you to describe yourself in one word, "awesome" typically will not land you the job.*

The date was May 7, 2009. It was graduation day at Miami University, more appropriately labeled "Doomsday" by my fellow Redhawks, who like myself, were now being dragged kicking and screaming out of the world of meal plans and frat parties—the best world that we have ever known —to the real world, the worst. The weather that day was dark and dreary, as were the job prospects for a recent college graduate with her master's degree in the ever so prestigious field of "Sports Studies." The economy was the worst its been since Hoovervilles were a thing, and the only offers I had received in the four months I'd been applying to jobs were $50 of free slot play at the local casino and an opportunity to join the bottom of a failing pyramid scheme, both of which left me in the red. Like most other highly educated people, I did not have much in the way of actual skills, and those that I did have were akin to those of a street performer: spinning a basketball on my finger, basic juggling, crafting the most beautiful origami the 5-year-olds at the YMCA have ever seen, and playing approximately 65% of several songs on the guitar. Was it hard to believe that employers would not have snatched somebody with such a diverse range of talent up long before graduation day? Apparently not to my parents, as they did not seem the least bit surprised to hear that I would be gracing them with my presence after a trip to Africa to climb Mt. Kilimanjaro and one last jobless summer in the college town that had taught me the exceptional value of dollar draft nights and free summer rent.

So there we were, my mother, my father, and I, sitting around the interrogation table, formerly known as our family dinner table, laying out options for my entrance into corporate America. Aspirations, aspirations, didn't really have any of those. Sure I wanted to be a ninja turtle for a brief period of time, then a hammock tester at a tropical resort, but after having dream after dream shattered by my elementary school teachers and "reality," I pretty much gave up the idea of ever joining the workforce. The only consistent ambition I've ever had is to rent jet skis out to people on the ocean. Not to own my own jet ski business, just to ride around on those dream machines all day telling people that their rental hour was up (a low aiming goal I attribute to being the youngest child). A few years down the road, I added driving the beer cart at a golf course and someone who shoots out free t-shirts to fans at sporting events to my career goals, but not much else. By the time I was 23 and finally ready for my first big girl job, it became apparent that *those* jobs were primarily doled out to high school seniors looking for gas and beer money. It became apparent that I would need to re-evaluate my life plan.

After applying to dozens of jobs online, whether or not they were looking to hire, it did not take long to realize that unless I was a registered nurse or Ryan Seacrest, my odds of getting a job were slim. I pursued every lead or callback I had gotten, including one sales job that dragged me along to shadow two, eight-hour days trekking all over southern Connecticut by foot to sell office supplies (which we carried with us) only to come to find that the salary was 100% commission and carried no benefits with it. Why they would not hire every single person that walked through their door is beyond me. Sure enough, I was not called back. It appears that my tertiary education was no match for the competitive world of stapler sales.

Typically, moving back in with one's parents—in contrast to the whole being frowned upon by society thing—brings the benefits of room *and* board. Yet this is where the Presser household strays from conventional models. The refrigerator consisted primarily of condiments, most of which expired while the Berlin Wall was still in one piece ("Lime juice doesn't go bad," my mom would reassure me). And with none of the butter knives being sharp enough for me to hunt my own food in the back yard, I was forced to take my mom up on her suggestion to sign up for a substitute teaching position at my old high school so that I could afford groceries. You see, among my mother's various odd jobs as an adult, which included manufacturing guns, working at a mini golf course, preparing taxes for H & R Block, writing for a local newspaper, and coaching a high school softball team, her newest endeavor was also substitute teaching, and reasoned that we would be able to carpool to work together...awesome.

Luckily, all that the Connecticut Department of Education requires of a substitute teacher is that they have a Bachelor's Degree and no criminal record. Check and mate! So it was settled, I would substitute teach at $85 a day for food money while continuing to pursue any and every career option I could. After the first class of sophomores I "taught," (or more aptly, pressed play on such exciting videos as *The Life and Times of the Mitochondria*, and *Glycolysis: The Movie!*) contained a girl who used to smear her own feces on the wall of the bathroom when I babysat her, I decided that a new source of income would be necessary. Listening to my former teachers' sexcapades in the faculty lounge further solidified my decision.

At some point in my incessant job search, I must have applied for a job on a cruise ship, or, several jobs on several cruise ships, as the case may have been. Of course I had no idea where or when I had ever applied to about 99% of the jobs I had heard back from (all told about four), but I was certainly in no position to care. What I *do* know is that a one "Javier Gonzalez" from the Seven Seas Group contacted me and asked if I would be available for an interview for a sports staff position with Royal Caribbean Cruise Lines on September 2, 2009.

"I'll have to clear my schedule."

And so there it was, my first interview for a job that I actually wanted. It's amazing how something as simple as "interest" in a job can completely alter one's approach to an interview. I did my research on Royal Caribbean and its affiliates, I selected action words that sort of described me from a list of traits that Miami's career services had told me employers appreciate, and I had even showered—all systems were go.

The interview lasted about twenty minutes and consisted of such questions as, "do you have any DUIs?" or "Do you have a problem working with foreigners?" While I passed those questions with flying colors, I had forgotten my selection on the application that said I spoke conversational French and Spanish. Whoops. What I *meant* to select was that I took six years of French in middle and high school and *should* definitely know conversational French, and while I've never actually taken a formal Spanish class, I do know how to order margaritas at *El Burrito Loco*, Oxford, Ohio's finest Mexican restaurant. So you can imagine my surprise when he asked if we could switch the conversation to French. I couldn't possibly imagine a situation that would elicit a response of "j'aime les croques monsieurs," which was the only French phrase that came to mind and was appropriate to say in front of children.

"Umm…it's been a while since I've used my French but I'm sure with a quick brush up it will all come back to me."

I neglected to mention that even if every piece of French that I learned did come back to me it *might* be enough to carry on an uneventful conversation with an elementary school child…a dumb elementary school child.

"Okay, ¿dónde aprendiste Éspañol?" he asked.

After I asked him to repeat himself, because he did not speak Spanish in a slow, patronizing manner that I so often rely on to comprehend the language, I responded with "a mi Universidad," which I guess technically was true. He asked me a few more questions in Spanish, which I answered with the same fluidity as O.J. Simpson in a murder trial, and believe it or not, asked me if I would be available for another Skype interview, this time with a woman from Royal Caribbean. Hoping my tone didn't indicate the surprise and disbelief in my voice, I kindly accepted another interview two days later.

I wore my nicest and only suit as I sat down in my bedroom, making sure everything within eyeshot of the webcam was appropriate for an interview. It was a little weird for a potential employer to see my bedroom the first time we meet, but it was the only quiet place in the house that a mouse had not been spotted in recent weeks, and I'm sure there was something about limiting the amount of vermin in your screenshot in the interview section of *What Color is Your Parachute*. At approximately 4 p.m. EST, a woman from Royal Caribbean dialed me up and we began to talk. Javier had not clicked on his video button when he Skyped me, so I followed his lead and did not click on mine. This lady, also neglected to show me her face, but asked me why she could not view me through my webcam.

"Oh I'm sorry," I said, giving her a visual of my face but still confused as to why she had not done the same.

There's something unsettling about somebody watching you when you can't see them, kind of like *The Truman Show*...or sharks. Is it not proper Skype etiquette to click on that little video button if you ask somebody else to? Technological improvements should not have to come at the expense of good manners. After what seemed like a successful interview (but then again so many of them do), I was worried that my hesitation to the question, "Are you willing to be a stilt walker in ship parades twice a week if necessary?" may have cost me the job. Rest assured, she offered me the sports staff position with Royal Caribbean the very next day. Finally! Employment that didn't involve getting people to sign up for something or breaking up fights at lunch duty.

I thought this was an appropriate time to look up what a member of the sport staff actually did. The website for the Seven Seas hiring partner described it as one who:

> ➢ Leads and participates in a variety of Sports Deck and Cruise Director activities and duties such as climbing wall, the surfing simulation pool aptly named "Flowrider," in-line skating, golf simulator, volleyball, basketball, golf course, ping pong, shuffle board, theme nights, spot lights, gangway, etc. (the "etc." meaning anything else they could

possibly need anybody for, you are fair game).

➢ Promotes and serves as Master of Ceremonies in Sports Deck activities, and Ship Shape programs (not quite sure when this job description was written but the company had suspended the Ship Shape bucks, fake money that could be redeemed for a free water bottle or t-shirt, before I had arrived. This caused quite a bit of disappointment to those loyal cruisers whose goal it seemed, was to accumulate as much free junk in one week as they possibly could, later to be pawned off as Christmas presents and eventually donated to the Salvation Army).

➢ Issues equipment to guests for: climbing wall, in-line skating, golf simulator, Flowrider, volleyball, basketball, golf course, ping pong, shuffleboard, etc. (there's that "et cetera" again).

➢ Explains and demonstrates proper use of apparatus and equipment for: climbing wall, in-line skating, golf simulator, Flowrider and any other related activities.

➢ Leads Ship Shape classes and events (again, this program was suspended by Royal Caribbean for what I was told were budget cutbacks due to the recession, despite their total equity of $6.8 billion reported in 2008).

➢ Organizes and conducts tournaments.

➢ May serve or participate as master of ceremonies

➢ Explains and demonstrates principles, techniques, and methods of regulating movement of body, hands, or feet to achieve proficiency in activity.

➢ Observes guests during activities to detect and correct mistakes.

From what I read, I was pretty confident that I could fulfill the duties of the job, and I accepted the offer. And from there, all common sense, logic, simplicity, and efficiency in making a living would cease.

First came endless confusion about my contract. Javier originally told me that the duration of the contract would be 6.75 months with a two-month vacation. Then came another email that stated 6.5 months with a two-week vacation. Then came a third email with yet another different contract length of five months with a six-week vacation. As I kept receiving these contradictory emails all I could think about was how grateful I was that Javier wasn't a doctor.

"Umm, it's diabetes you have. No wait, I think it's a tumor. Now that I look closer at it I'm pretty sure it's jaundice. Oh snap, it was actually diabetes the whole time, that's what I guessed first, remember?"

The contract, after I asked Javier to confirm it with Royal Caribbean, was for six months and three weeks, at which point I would be given a new ship assignment that I would begin after a two-month vacation if I so chose. It carried with it an incredible $1,700 monthly salary (which I realize is less than half of what my colleagues were making, but still more money than I had ever touched at once), free room and board, and emergency medical coverage (although the ship's medical center turned out to be a bigger joke than Ross Perot's campaign for presidency, but I'll get to that later). I was told by Javier that I would be responsible for paying for my own flight out to join the ship, which would be to either Virginia or Miami, and I would be given at least two weeks notice before I had to start.

The next step of the process was to sit and wait for a ship assignment, which I was told could be between two weeks and five months (and I thought the gap the cable repairman gave me was long). Sigh. It was looking like I would have to find some sort of a job in the meantime. I had somehow managed to get a job at Philips Remote Cardiac Services as a clinical cardiac assistant, which sounds much more impressive than it was. Sixteen hours a week at $12 an hour, I was responsible for calling pacemaker recipients and running EKG tests on their hearts through the phone, or at least I would have been, had I ever seen the first day of work. Evidently, Philips didn't feel confident entrusting clients' hearts to people like myself, so the job required a three-week training course. The nerd in me found it really interesting. I'd taken a class at Miami about EKG interpretation, but couldn't really concentrate past the sweaty, shirtless 20-something athletes we always had performing the VO2 Max tests. The middle-aged woman teaching the training course this go around made it much easier to focus on the slides.

While I was driving home from my second to last day of training, on Wednesday, October 14, I received a call from Javier informing me that I had been given a ship assignment.

"You have been assigned to the *Voyager of the Seas*. You are to join on Sunday, October 18 in Barcelona."

Excited that this job wasn't a scam, but also confused because this information contradicted everything I had been told (2 weeks notice at least, and a flight to Miami or Virginia), I expressed my concern that a last minute flight to Barcelona would probably cost more than my first month's salary. I also told him that I needed to give my employer more notice than 4 days. In reality, I had bought a flight out to Ohio for homecoming weekend at Miami for the weekend of the 24-25th, the only time it's socially acceptable for the 23+ population to relive their glory days.

"The earliest I can possibly leave is October 27," I lamented to Javier.

"Okay, I will send you your letter of employment and RCI will help you find a flight for the 27th."

Next objective, break the news to the only job I'd ever worked that stood potential to be a real adult career and tell them I was quitting before technically starting, in order to rent out skates on a ship for what would amount to $5.61 an hour and not a single day off for nearly seven months. Before labeling me the "World's Worst Decision Maker," I did have my reasons for choosing the gag gift of the employment world:

1. *Titanic* was one of my favorite movies.
2. I kept envisioning the countless jokes I could make with the term "seamen"
3. It would be very similar to college without the classes or homework.

If those weren't enough, and I can't imagine why they wouldn't be enough, then it also afforded me the opportunity to travel, meet new people, and create more adventures in a few months than many people experience in their entire lives. Packing up your whole life in an oversized duffel bag, leaving all of your friends and family behind, not sure when you will be able to talk to them next, and not knowing a single soul as you set out for the great unknown with reckless abandon incited feelings of romanticism, coupled with an adrenaline rush and angst. It was not the first time I had taken such a chance in life. I had done it when I went to Ohio for college knowing neither what to expect nor a single person, and also when I had opted to study abroad on the other side of the planet in Australia. And, while I was not permitted to ride a kangaroo to class, after several ensuing debates with campus security, I still managed to have the best five months of my life. Rumor has it that if you're willing to take a chance, the view from the other side is spectacular, I was just hoping that the other side didn't turn out to be a present day remake of the slave ship story *Amistad.*

# CHAPTER II: A BILLION DOLLAR MONOPOLY

*Lesson I've learned the hard way #31: I will never be wealthy enough to own a cruise ship.*

Tourism continues to be the largest service sector industry in the world, and cruising is the fastest-growing section by far. It's like the New York Yankees of the service industry: controlled by the hands of few, yet generating ridiculous amounts of money. Despite the economic turmoil that was 2009, cruise lines still posted profits to their $40 billion industry.[1] What's more incredible is that over 90% of the industry's passenger capacity is in the hands of just three families, and nearly half of it belongs to Carnival's chairman and CEO Mickey Arison.[2] You may have seen him on the sidelines cheering on his team, the *Miami Heat,* because where's the fun in owning dozens of luxurious cruise ships when you can own some of the best basketballs player in the world? Okay, I guess those would both be pretty awesome. As would ranking in the top 100 of *Forbes* richest people in the world with a net worth of $6.1 billion. I signed up for a student checking account last year in order to receive a free pizza, and Mickey Arison is laughing off a $500,000 fine for tweeting about the NBA lockout—literally, he was fined for tweeting "LOL" after somebody asked him what

---

[1] Garin, Kristoffer A. *Devils on the Deep Blue Sea.*
[2] Ibid.

he thought about Clipper's owner Donald Sterling. Pretty harsh punishment, but good to know it won't do too much damage to his #94 ranking.

What's interesting about the Arison family, is that Ted, the man who started the Carnival Corporation, and in doing so would succeed in making sure his son never had to work a day in his life, also had a daughter who resides in Israel. He decided that she was worth only 35% of his possessions, which is why Shari Arison embarrassingly only makes the cut for the top 200 wealthiest people in the world.[3] Psh, $5.1 billion may be impressive for a woman in the Middle East, but she's not even the richest one in her family! I'm the 4th richest person in *my* family…my immediate family…fifth if you count half of my dad's wealth for my mom. Shari Arison did manage to make #56 of the "200 Greatest Israelis" list, conspicuously beating out Moses, King David, and Jesus. Alright, so I guess she's doing alright for herself, but only leaving your youngest daughter 35% of your assets is still a dick move. Jay Presser, please note.

In the summer of 2006, a tenacious and helpful man by the name of Kristoffer A. Garin took it upon himself to write a book titled *Devils on the Deep Blue Sea*, complete with research and statistics about, as luck would have it, the *Voyager of the Seas*. For the purposes of this book, we're going to go ahead and assume that anything this Harvard grad researched and published is going to

---

[3] Vinton, K. (2016). Meet the Richest Billionaires in the Middle East.

be way more in-depth and accurate than anything I would've found on my own before losing interest. And I would like to go ahead and credit him with a good amount of what follows in this section.

The *Voyager of the Seas* was built in Finland in 1999 and at that time, it was the largest passenger vessel ever constructed, beating the previous record holder, the *Grand Princess*, by nearly 33%. She stretches 1,021 feet in length, almost exactly the height of the Eiffel Tower, or about three times the height of the Luxor hotel and casino if that reference is more beneficial to your tastes. That's about 140 ft longer than the *RMS Titanic* and nearly 10 tons heavier, although *it* manages to stay afloat (sorry Captain Smith that was a cheap shot, the *Voyager* doesn't even *attempt* to sail through iceberg alley[4]).

The behemoth has a maximum capacity of 3,838 passengers with another 1,170 or so crewmembers to weigh her down. And weigh her down they do. The passengers alone are responsible for nearly three hundred tons and, it is estimated, will collectively gain another fifteen tons on their weeklong cruise. Over 160,000 meals will be served up, requiring at least five tons of meat, seven hundred gallons of ice cream, and nearly five thousand bottles of wine, one thousand bottles of hard liquor, and twenty thousand cans of beer. Those numbers are obviously not inclusive of the crew bar, where I could swear I've seen nearly twenty thousand cans of beer consumed in one party.[5]

---

[4] Garin, p. 4-11.

Passengers can delight in throwing up all that food and drink in one of the *Voyager's* three pools, seven hot tubs, 10,000 square foot solarium, or all three as I have had the pleasure of witnessing. For the food connoisseur, there are three formal dining rooms, a super formal dining room, and for those with a classier taste in food, Johnny Rockets. There's also a buffet in case you're one of those people who prefers to think that walking to the buffet troughs yourself cancels out any of the food consumed in them—because the fact is, there is never any limit to any of the food a passenger can order. I've seen one guest order and finish an entire family of lobsters after consuming two courses prior.

Guests have the option to wash it all down at one of seventeen bars. That's sixteen more than my hometown in a space a fraction of the size. Like Suffield, CT, the *Voyager* has only one library, mostly occupied with the plus sixty crowd trying to keep their minds sharp with a daily sudoku. And what mobile town isn't complete without a rock wall, inline skating track, full sized basketball court, mini golf course, gym with steam room and sauna, spa, musical theater, and the backbone of any good ship—an ice skating rink? Slightly more morbid, but no less important, is the morgue that some will be surprised to learn exists in the bowels of the ship for all of those elderly passengers looking for one last hurrah, or those who overdid it at the cheeseburger buffet.

---

[5]Garin, p. 6.

But these areas that offer the revelry and opulence of a weeklong cruise to guests are strictly off limits to the majority of the nearly 1,200 crewmembers onboard, most of who have to travel the much blander "I-95" hallway instead of the more glamorous Royal Promenade that guests are accustomed to. As if we weren't already aware that we were second-rate citizens, they have to label our designated hallway after a congested and polluted highway whose news stories are most often associated with debilitating auto accidents. Tractor-trailers just don't crash on things labeled "The Royal Promenade."

The worst part of traveling the I-95 wasn't the fear of slipping on the often-wet floors, or the lackluster white paint that encovered it, or even the idea that you had to play a lifelike version of Frogger when it was stacked with luggage carts shifting back and forth on a rocky sea day. Those all pale in comparison to the rancid smell of the I-95. You better believe a seasoned veteran on the *Voyager* would know the specific areas in the hallway to breathe out of their mouth to keep from gagging. The first area obviously being the trash room. If you've ever tried to mask the smell of rotten eggs with feces and tuna fish, you might have an idea of what this room smelled like. Which is why trips to take the garbage "out" were always determined by a nerve-racking game of Rocks, Paper, Scissors with my roommate.

Another notoriously noxious spot was the refrigeration complex, where all the uncooked food on the ship was held. I'm not quite sure how pineapples and lettuce managed to create such a foul odor, but it did concern me that those foods would be in the staff mess hall days after none of the guests wanted them. And unbelievably the smell gets worse. The final place nose plugs would've been helpful was in the aft of the ship just below the bathroom in the crew bar. It had a tendency to overflow on occasion, and one of my coworkers had the unfortunate luck to receive a golden shower while standing directly under it. For those of you who do not know what a golden shower is, it is not a lucrative as it sounds.

So this was the ship on which I was to spend the next 6.75 months of my life, as I assisted cruisers more than willing to pad the pockets of these wealthy families for a weeklong escape from their shitty little lives in an even shittier economy. Luckily for me, I wasn't aware just yet how much shit would rain down on me simply getting onboard.

# CHAPTER III: GETTING OVER THERE

*Lesson I've Learned the hard way #48: Communicating with somebody thousands of miles away in a language not native to him via email is not as seamless as you may think.*

So that was it. There was only a flight to Europe standing between me and the next adventure...or so I thought. Javier had sent me a bunch of paperwork, most of which I couldn't fill out until he gave me the necessary information (such as my ship assignment, my scheduled flight information, confirming that I had seen the "Life Aboard" video he has never sent, etc.), which begged the obvious question of, why not wait until I have that information before sending me the new hire checklist? After the three days of notice he wanted to give me to join the ship, my question was answered. The paperwork Javier sent me also contained a 36-page "Getting Onboard" download that contained rules so specific it would make anyone question how crewmembers follow them all. Alas, after my first hour on the ship, I realized 99% of employees do not. Some of the excerpts from this ridiculous rulebook include:

*While on duty, uniforms must be clean, pressed, and in good repair at all times. Your undergarments may not be seen through your uniform. Your supervisor may use his/her judgment and request a change in any aspect of your appearance.

*Astoundingly, a giant sunshine costume and Tiki head did not merit changing.*

*Body art such as visible branding is not acceptable. Body piercings other than one piercing in each earlobe, are not acceptable. Tattoos must not be offensive to our guests or coworkers and should not be visible.

*If they are not visible to guests then why can't they be offensive?*

*Shoes should be polished and kept in good repair. You should wear socks that are the same color as your shoes when in uniform. Women should wear flesh-colored hosiery when wearing skirts in uniform.

*No matter how many times I tried, my sneakers never reflected the shine of the polish.*

*Females may wear a single earring in each earlobe that is a simple, matched pair of gold, silver or a color that blends with the uniform. Earrings should be no larger than 2.4 cm or 15/16th of an inch in diameter. Men may not wear earrings while in guest areas. *Leave any earrings that measure a full inch at home: check.*

*In addition, you may wear one ring per hand, a business-style watch and conservative tie clip while on duty. All other visible jewelry may not be worn while on duty.

*Apparently a neon orange watch qualifies as "business-style" these days.*

\*Nails should be clean, neatly manicured to an even length, and not longer than the tip of the fingers and thumb. Women can wear clear or colored nail polish that matches the uniform. Designs on nails are not appropriate when in guest areas.
*You hear that ladies? Make sure you scrape off those designs from your nails when you walk into a guest area.*

\*Male employees are to keep their sideburns trimmed and no longer than the bottom of the earlobe. A well-trimmed beard or moustache is acceptable so long as the beard or moustache is fully-grown at sign-on. Females whose underarms or legs are exposed while on duty are to keep their underarms and legs clean-shaven when in uniform.
*This rule reminded me of the American classic* Footloose; *if we let the sideburns grow lower than the ear lobe who knows what chaos will ensue next?*

\*Your hair and scalp should always be clean. Hair must be dry when reporting to duty. Please do not comb, brush, or arrange your hair in the presence of guests.
*Is there only half of a penalty if your scalp is dirty but your hair is clean? And it's awfully difficult to report to duty with dry hair when you were just swimming with dolphins and returned to the ship*

*with barely enough time to change into your uniform and sprint to the fourteenth floor just to show up to work on time.*

*Hair accessories should be business-like and coordinate with the uniform. All hair accessories are subject to the approval of your immediate supervisor. Wigs, hairpieces, and hair extensions must be tasteful and appear natural.
*I have yet to see a hairpiece that appears natural.*

Another set of ship rules randomly enforced by the "Master," known as a Captain to everybody but himself, are as follows:

## Master's Rules & Regulations
These rules are the commonly accepted code of ship operations. Each master onboard our ships has the authority to establish his rules and regulations, and may be different from the ones listed below. By joining our company, you are agreeing that you will live by these rules while working for Royal Caribbean International or Celebrity Cruises, whether onboard or ashore.
1. No drunkenness will be tolerated.
2. No officer, staff or employee will possess or use illegal drugs or weapons.
3. No indecent language will be used.
4. No employee will be involved in brawls or fights.
5. Only officers and staff are permitted to be in public areas when off duty.
6. Employees will not deface, abuse or steal the ship's property.

7. Respect must be given to officers at all times.

8. Respect and courtesy must be given to guests at all times.

9. All shipboard employees must attend boat drills and other required safety drills.

10. Shipboard employees must report for duty on time.

11. Shipboard employees must retain the cabins assigned to them and may make changes only with permission from the head of their division.

12. When on shore or leave, all shipboard employees must report aboard ship a half-hour before sailing and one hour when tendering.

13. All shipboard employees must show their crew cards upon boarding the ship.

14. Shipboard employees must be properly dressed at all times.

15. Mealtime schedules must be followed.

16. Shipboard employees will not miss the ship.

17. Gambling is prohibited for all shipboard employees.

18. Smoking in bed is absolutely prohibited.

With the exception of #13 and #16, I have personally seen all of these rules broken on our ship dozens of times. Granted, the crewmember that slugged a guest after a bad combination of Mexican medication and alcohol was unfortunately let go, but very few of the other violations have resulted in disciplinary action. My guess is that the rules are there as vindication, if somebody with authority wants you off the ship, they have a plethora of reasons to fire you if they so choose.

After familiarizing myself with the code of conduct, I had the brilliant idea to look up the itinerary of the *Voyager of the Seas* and see what utopian hotspots I would be gracing with my presence for the next seven months. Okay, my sister actually had the idea and told me where it went, but I went online to confirm it. Her story checked out. From the time I would be joining the ship, it would depart from Barcelona, Spain, then head to Naples, Italy, Civitavecchia (Rome), Italy, Livorno (Florence), Italy,[6] Villefranche, France, and Marseille, France, with only one sea day in between, the agony of which would only be realized after experiencing the misery of working on a sea day.

While years earlier I had the pleasure of visiting Naples in the midst of one of their infamous sanitation strikes, I couldn't help but feel that watching people throw bags of garbage, or furniture, or feral animals out of their third story apartments reflected poorly on the birthplace of pizza, and I was more than willing to give good old Napoli another shot. I had been to Rome on three separate occasions before, but I was sure the Eternal City was much more interesting when you actually splurged for entrance fees. "There's nothing left inside the Coliseum, if you want to see *that* watch *Gladiator*," my mother would respond when her children surprisingly showed interest in an historical relic. Odd, coming from the same woman who dragged us on a three-hour

---

[6] Rome and Florence are in parentheses because the actual cities are an hour and a half away from the ports on a good day.

wild goose chase in 100-degree weather through Mt. Vesuvius in search of petrified corpses. I visited the Tuscan region of Italy once, and once was all it took to fall in love with it. At the heart of it all is Florence, its capital city, and one of the most beautiful in the world. Home to Michelangelo's *David*, the most magnificent piece of artwork I have ever laid eyes on, and much more impressive than the tiny, bland bust of that hussy Mona Lisa (sorry Leonardo it's true, and you were my least favorite Ninja Turtle as well). I may or may not have developed an unhealthy obsession with the man and the legend according to my friends, but I was fairly certain that all of the other women at the Accademia were just as frustrated that Mr. Right was a marble statue from hundreds of years ago…maybe not.

Rest assured, my exciting new adventure wouldn't solely consist of revisiting places I'd already been. My friends and I had never made it to Barcelona after we were gypsied out of most of our belongings in Granada, Spain, the previous New Year's Eve, and our high school French teacher opted to add Monte Carlo to the school trip's itinerary only after those of us most likely to wind up at a Gambler's Anonymous meeting had graduated (I still don't see a problem with betting on French Pictionary). Sadly, my feet would never touch down on the prostitute-laden streets of Marseille. Incredibly enough, despite Marseille being chosen as a port of call, the weather was "too rough" to dock there three of the four weeks I was there (and I had training the only time we ever did). What was even more impressive was that the

Captain would often announce the weather was too rough to dock days in advance. Even more unbelievable was that, at least on one occasion, the water was more tranquil than that time my friends and I foolishly decided go sailing in Cape Cod and ended up having to paddle our way back due to the lack of wind—it was calm.

While one could do worse than to visit the same destinations in Europe every week, I was glad the itinerary also called for a repositioning cruise to the Caribbean. Not only because every single person I tried to speak French to answered me in English, nor because toward the end of the summer the weather in Europe started to resemble that of New England, which I had longed to escape from, but because the U.S. dollar was worth little over half of a Euro. The last time I was in France the dollar was worth six francs, and there was nothing I hated more than seeing France's economy surpass ours. Surely the failing economies of the Caribbean would bring relief to my suffering wallet.

Stops on the crossing included Cartageña, Spain, Madeira, Portugal, Tenerife, Canary Islands, Nassau, Bahamas, and finally, the highly anticipated Galveston, Texas. This Atlantic Crossing would be completed over the span of two weeks, meaning there would be eight sea days—six of them in a row—as we would cross what seemed like an endless expanse of water, all the while counting our blessings that there were no ice bergs or pirates en route. But all of that was still much further out of sight than I could have imagined.

In addition to the Getting Onboard packet, Javier also sent me a new hire checklist, a Life Insurance Beneficiary form, the Master's Rules and Regulations form, a Shipboard drug and alcohol policy form, two RCI application forms (confusing, as I had already been offered the job, and contained questions I had answered in the interviews as well as a request for references), New Hire Data Sheet, a list of things I would need for my uniform (about 50% of which proved to be accurate for me), and four medical forms. The medical forms, which I was told were absolutely compulsory for boarding the ship, demanded nearly everything short of a rectal exam. Don't get me wrong, I was more than thankful for that, but polio and small pox had been all but eradicated in the United States since the 1950s, and if my insurance company doesn't deem it worthy to cover the cost of chest X-Rays for a physical, then I don't deem the threat of pneumonia worthy of my substitute teaching money either. Alas, I will go into further detail about the crack medical system Royal Caribbean has later, where I can give it the kind of accolades it deserves.

Like many other jobs, Royal Caribbean requires a background check of its potential employees. Unlike many other jobs, I'm not sure they *actually* care if you do have a record, so long as they don't know about it. My hypothesis was influenced by a few aspects of the application process.

First off, I was offered a ship assignment before I had even gotten a background check, and could have been the second gunmen on the grassy knoll for all they knew. I had however, been fingerprinted to teach at Miami University in 2007, completed a more extensive fingerprinting session for a Peace Corps application in 2009, and yet another one in order to substitute teach a few months later. Now, perhaps I have a misconception of the function that fingerprints serve in this world, but I was under the impression that a national background check meant that your fingerprints were in a national database to which police had access. This would be helpful if one commits a crime in one state, and tries to substitute teach, for instance, in another. My local police department does not subscribe to this method, and assured me that they could not look up my past fingerprints. So once again, after being fingerprinted four times in the past year (twice by my local police department in two weeks), I made a copy and sent it to Javier about four days before I was to fly to Rome. Within an hour of sending the email, I received a reply from him saying "the criminal background check does not say if there are any records under your name, do you have the paper where it says that your record is clear?" I guess fingerprints are even more useless than I thought.

I returned to the police station for the fourth time in two weeks, which was enough for every dispatcher to recognize me as "the fingerprint girl," and ask upon entering if I needed more fingerprints taken. While I was happy to report that I did not need yet another set of fingerprints taken, I do not think I gained any credibility when I asked, "Umm...do you have a piece of paper that says I'm not a criminal?"

"What do you mean?" the dispatcher questioned.

"I just need a piece of paper that says I don't have a record."

"Like a background check? Isn't that what you got fingerprints for?"

*No, those were just for fun,* I felt like telling her, *they're actually framed in my room right now next to my two useless diplomas.*

"Is there any way I can just get a piece of paper saying I don't have a record?"

"Do you want a statewide search or a local search?"

Well since I haven't lived in Connecticut in the past six years, the six years where I would've been the most likely to actually acquire a police record, I replied with, "Statewide will be fine."

"Okay you need to drive to Hartford for that."

Hmm... that would be another twenty-minute drive, and I hadn't set the DVR to record the *Sixteen and Pregnant* marathon that was on that day. "Alright, just give me a local one then."

"It'll be ready in about three business days, but if you're gonna need more fingerprints you should do them now while Bill is here."

"I'm all set, thanks," I retorted. What the hell is a business day for a police station anyway? Batman doesn't stop fighting crime on weekends.

My record was ready after five normal human business days, not three, and when I picked it up, it was simply a piece of paper that had two boxes that could be checked. One of the boxes read "Record found," and the other, "No record found." That was it?! No fancy police stamp or paw print from the K-9 unit? Just a manually checked box stating that I didn't have (or rather they couldn't find) a record in a town of 14,000 people. I've made more official documents on Print Shop Deluxe in third grade. Surely, if fingerprints weren't good enough for Javier then this wouldn't be. I emailed it to him with the expectation that it would be ripped apart for lack of credibility and the fact that it only covers a town roughly the same size as three Royal Caribbean ships. But, to my consternation, this was all that was required in a background check of Royal Caribbean employees—good thing there would be cameras everywhere on the ship.

By October 21st, all of my paperwork had been approved by Javier, which was good, considering the letter of employment I was sent had me scheduled to join the ship by October 28. And, as if our correspondences weren't confusing enough, another hiring agent working for the same company, José, began to email me information as well, such as my official ship assignment information, port agent phone numbers and names, and my letter of employment. When I asked about booking a last minute flight, Javier said he would ask RCI if they would help with the ticket. Shortly thereafter, he notified me that they would pay for the flight to Rome. Shortly after that, José told me that they wouldn't. RCI would book the flight and pay for it, but then I would have to pay it back onboard once I had received my first paycheck.

"RCI was offering to pay for the flights if you were to join sooner," his email read. This flight would comprise nearly my entire monthly paycheck and it was scheduled a day before I would even be in Connecticut. I felt obligated to send José an email laced with exclamation points to get my message across more clearly:

When did you ever tell me that I would have to pay for my flight to Rome?! I was under the impression that Royal Caribbean was paying, because that is exactly what Javier told me. I am a little concerned about the lack of communication. Also I TOLD Javier CLEARLY that I would not be able to LEAVE CT until October 27, and this flight is for the 26th when I'll be in Ohio!

His response, verbatim:

Dear Deedee,
I am not happy with the tone of your email, specially coming from someone who is just about to join a company which it stands for Service and Excellence. When I spoke to you I clearly told you, and when I said I clearly told is because I never offer to any crewmember that Royal Caribbean would paid for their joining ticket unless that is case or if the position entitles it. In your case Royal Caribbean was offering the airline ticket if you had joined last weekend.

You may recall that I told you that
Royal Caribbean would assist with your
airline ticket and you would paid back
once onboard and that is exactly what
I communicated to Amanda Chalmers -
Casting Specialist.
I do not think there has been any lack
of communication. We can request your
departure date to be changed to the
27th October, as that is the date you
told me you could travel, so that you
can join in the 28th.
Thank you.
Best regards,

José Rodriguez
The Seven Seas Group


After reading and rereading one of the
more confusing emails that the Seven Seas Dream
Team had sent me, I came to the conclusions that:

> 1. Exclamation points and using all caps
> helps convey the same meaning in other
> cultures and,

> 2. I would still be able to join the *Voyager*,
> although I would no longer be granted the
> luxury of a few hours of rest after
> traversing the Atlantic and beginning my
> first day of work.

A few more days passed with me checking
my email furiously to see if I had been sent a new
itinerary, you know, one that I would actually be
able to use. And then it came. On Monday,
October 26th, at 3:00 p.m. I finally received my
new itinerary, less than 24 hours in advance of my
flight, but at least it was for the correct date and
you've really got to choose your battles with these

hiring partners. My flight left from Hartford at 1:50 p.m. October 27th, had a layover in D.C., and was scheduled to arrive in Rome at 7:25 a.m. on Wednesday October 28th. My letter of employment required that I be at the ship by 11:00 a.m. on October 28th, and God only knows what happens if you're late. With the organizational zeal of which Italian airports operate, I knew it would take no less than an hour to get out of there, and the port was about a 90-minute drive from the airport. It would be cutting it close, but instead of worrying, I decided that they were professionals who had done this a multitude of times and I would put my trust in them. *Big* mistake.

# CHAPTER IV: NEVER TRUST A TRAVEL AGENT

*Lesson I've learned the hard way #67: When a hiring agent for a cruise ship assures you that "somebody" will be at the airport to greet and drive you 1.5 hours to the ship, do not believe him.*

The flight from Hartford to D.C. had gone smoothly enough. I was thankful to see that United Airlines hadn't yet enacted a baggage fee for international flights, as I checked a single bag for the next seven months of my life. I was also thankful that Bradley International Airport has never taken me more than 20 minutes to get from the entrance to my terminal. I landed at Dulles and phoned my friends and family for what would be the last time in a while.

The last of us, and I was the last of "us," boarded the plane about an hour ahead of our scheduled take off time. Everything seemed to be running smoothly; no giant lizards about to rip us out of the sky, no box cutters in sight, all systems were go. Then the announcement came.

"We're very sorry but there appears to be a problem with the plane's air conditioning. We're going to need to get somebody on here to fix this."

I'm not sure whom they got to fix the system, although it was somebody in the immediate surrounding area who was chosen to save time. After about thirty minutes they explained the problem had been fixed and encouraged us to give the mysterious saviors a round of applause. They assured us that we had not lost our place in the line as we pulled away from the gate about to take off. Then they realized that the system had broken again. Well done boys. Your repair job lasted all of ten minutes. Driving back to the gate, United decided that perhaps it would be a good idea if we actually waited for a real maintenance team before sending the twenty-ton mass of steel into the air.

By this time, we had been sitting on a plane with no circulating air for about two hours, and they were not about to let us get off—we tried. Nor were the flight attendants particularly friendly when anybody had the audacity to request a cup of water. My iPod had been dead since the first 20 minutes of my first flight; apparently my environmentally-conscious friend who was over the house to say goodbye, had turned off my power strip while I was attempting to charge it. She was sorry, but I was out of options for avoiding conversation.

As it turned out, the couple next to me was flying out to rejoin a Holland America ship as nurses. We chatted about all kinds of things, the darker side of ship life, the lighter side of ship life, and how Holland America was kind enough to pay for all of its employees' flights, new hires and all. The delightful conversation was a nice distraction from the lack of oxygen and the increasingly warm temperature in the cabin.

In fact, the plane was now ready to take off for a third time when somebody had noticed an unresponsive woman who had passed out in the row in front of me. Her friend came back from the bathroom to inform everybody that she had simply taken a Xanax and chased it with wine because she was nervous to fly. I can't imagine why this flight would have made her nervous. Unfortunately, this was after somebody had summoned a flight attendant who felt it was necessary to drive back into the gate yet again and have the older woman inspected by medics. Another half hour passed before the EMT squad came to the same conclusion as everybody else.

Three hours after our scheduled departure time, we finally had taken off. If I was cutting it close before, this little three-hour setback squandered any chance I had of making it to the ship on time. Now I'm not exactly the worrying type, but I had no idea what time the ship left the port, who was picking me up, and my Italian was worse than my French, so figuring this information out would be slightly more challenging. Surely whoever was picking me up would check the flight delays and see that my plane would be arriving three hours later, right?

Instead of worrying about something I couldn't change, I decided to take United up on their very generous offer of one free alcoholic beverage for the three-hour delay. Sure, free alcohol may come standard on most decent international flights, but United makes up for their lack of privileges with their superior air conditioning maintenance. It seemed as if circulating air *and* a working TV screen were asking for too much, so the next several hours were going to be longer than anticipated.

Sleeping was not an option as I had continued my unfortunate airplane streak of sitting in between a snorer and the loudest baby in America. Obviously the baby had not capitalized on the complimentary drink. When the snorer was awake the baby was crying, when the baby was asleep, the snorer was doing what he did best. It was as if the travel gods were conspiring to make this the worst flight of my life. Nice try bastards, but *that* honor is reserved for any time I fly Alitalia Airlines.

After about nine hours of staring at the seat in front of me, the plane finally touched down in the Italian capital. I collected my luggage at around 11:00 a.m., the time I was supposed to be boarding the ship, and my heart was nearly beating out of my chest with nervous anticipation combined with the very good possibility that nobody would be on the other side of the doors to greet me. I had given Javier the benefit of the doubt when I had asked what to do when I get off the plane. "Somebody will be there to greet you," I was told no less than three times. Javier's communication skills up to this point had not given me much confidence, but what choice did I have? The whole idea of working on a cruise was a leap of faith—not knowing any details just added to the allure. And, unfortunately, the stress.

As I walked out of the baggage claim area and the moment of truth had arrived, I was thankful. Thankful that Javier's incompetence thus far had prepared me for the incredible frustration, disappointment, and anxiety I was now feeling. I scanned and lapped the entire room about five times, looking for any trace of a human looking for me. I wasn't sure if the port agent, or a Royal Caribbean staff, or a Seven Seas rep was picking me up, I didn't even know if those were all the same thing. I *did* know that there was not a single sign with my name on it anywhere to be seen in the airport and that I was already late. Typically, be it a result of my overly trusting nature or just pure laziness, I throw my faith into any authoritative organization—schools, banks, multimillion-dollar corporations—but I was glad I opted to hedge my bets this one time. I had actually written down the port agent's phone number, in the "slim" possibility that anything would not go according to the ever-so-detailed plan.

I interrupted what seemed to be a very passionate conversation between two very flirtatious rental car agents to ask the price of the shuttle to the Civitavecchia's port. Noticeably annoyed after I had the nerve to ask a work related question during work hours, the woman responded, "150 euro."

Oh great, 150 euro. 150 euro!? Unless the U.S. dollar had made a miraculous recovery in the time I had been on the plane (which wasn't out of the question given the length of time I was on that godforsaken plane), that was nearly $300! I could've flown to Sweden for cheaper than that. After about five minutes of complaining to the cuddly co-workers, I felt that we were good enough friends to ask them if I could borrow their phone. I took out the two port agents' numbers that I had pried out of Javier. To me they looked more like complicated math equations than telephone numbers. The phone I was dialing on obviously thought so as well, as all I got was a "this number does not exist, please check the ridiculously long number and try again," recording (at least that's what I imagine it said, my Italian was not perfect). I had one of the workers try to connect with a human on the other end. No dice. The first number did not exist. Once again my only option was to give Javier the benefit of the doubt and assume it was a simple typo. I tried the second number. A man answered in Italian. I asked for the port agent. He hung up. I tried for a second time, once again enlisting the help of the rental car worker and her incredible grasp of the Italian language. "No answer," she said. "Now if you will excuse us we need to pay attention to our actual customers."

Looking around and seeing nobody within 10 feet of the counter, I understood what she really needed to pay attention to. I also noticed that one of the pay phones had opened up. The three successive times I called were about as successful as Paris Hilton's movie career. I then discovered that a taxi to the port would cost about 90 euro; better, but still not in the price range I was willing to pay for RCI's incompetence. I told those clowns thanks, but no thanks. Next, there was an Egyptian man who suggested I take his friend's taxi because it would be cheaper. Whether he offered this out of genuine concern or to sell me into the sex slave trade remains a mystery. I took his "business card," which consisted of his name and phone number on a piece of construction paper—hand cut construction paper—but sadly forgot to email him the details of where I would be for the next couple of weeks as he had requested.

Finally, I asked a tour guide in the airport who actually looked like he knew what the word "organization" meant, and he suggested taking the train—two trains actually. I had been told (by the Egyptian of course) that the train cost 100 euro and was very unreliable. The tour guide, or, my new best friend, estimated the train would cost about 10 euro. Sold.

To the train station I went; with about 70 lbs of luggage and eyes that were bloodshot beyond belief. I should also mention that by the time I caught the first train to the port, it was past noon and I had no idea if the ship was still sitting in it. I assumed that they would give people a sufficient amount of time in the Roman port since it was so damn far and inconvenient to get to, but assuming things had not served me well thus far. I was also hoping the train would drop me off right outside the ship's door. This would not be the case, and after getting off the second train an hour and a half later, I realized objects in my bloody eyeshot are farther than they appear. Much farther.

I exited the train station and looked around for that beautiful body of water they call the Mediterranean Sea. Finding the boardwalk after a surprisingly short struggle, I saw ships in the distances to both sides of me and opted to go in the direction opposite the fishing boats and oil tankers. After what couldn't have been less than two miles of schlepping my suitcase, guitar, and backpack in a coat and jeans in nearly 80-degree weather, I had arrived at the *Voyager's* doorstep. Needless to say, I was sweating profusely (the gray shirt was a poor choice) when I arrived over two hours late to my first real job after college, making what can only be described as a truly Presser-esque impression. I'm not sure if I was more relieved to find that the ship was still there, or that the opportunity to sleep seemed so very close. That of course was until the rude awakening I would get upon boarding the *M.S. Voyager of the Seas*.

# CHAPTER V: WHAT DID I GET MYSELF INTO?

*Lesson I've learned the hard way #81: Do not, under any circumstances, assume that proper training will be provided before beginning a job where people's lives are at stake.*

I can remember boarding the ship like it was yesterday. After showing the security guard at the gangway my passport and employment papers, I was greeted by a friendly South African woman from the crew office. She led me through a maze of crew areas, strictly off limits to guests, and took me to read and sign my contract for the first time. I was curious if anybody had ever flown across the globe to join a ship and refused to sign the contract; you're not exactly in a position to negotiate at that point, after all. Brilliant on their part really, if I were them I would've added all kinds of wacky clauses to that contract like, "You have to clean the poop deck after there's been an accident," or, "If we are taken over by pirates you agree to be sacrificed," but I guess that could be encompassed in the part of the contract that states, "...and wherever else your assistance is needed." Exactly what this clause would entail would be experienced that first night.

As I looked over the contract I only noticed a few errors, such as my social security number, which didn't have a single number correct, and the fact that my zip code only had 4 digits listed. Right below that, I noticed that it listed my monthly guaranteed pay as $1,700, and my monthly vacation pay as $132. I guess this is my fault for assuming that when Javier told me I would be paid $1,700 a month with two months of paid vacation, he meant I would be paid the same amount for my vacation pay. You know, kind of like the way paid holidays and paid vacations mean you're paid as if you were there—the same amount. Perhaps I could've lived off of $33 a week in the Philippines, but it would be considerably more difficult in America. I would cross that bridge when I came to it, I thought as I put my John Hancock on the last page, and in so doing, became the *Voyager of the Seas'* newest employee.

The man who was to be my supervisor took over from there. Pablo, a Brazilian in his mid-30s, introduced me to what would be my living quarters for the next seven months of my life. About half the size of my freshman dorm room in college, the cabin was the smallest possible space you could imagine two people living in for any amount of time. We'll call it "cozy." Unlike my dorm room, it did have a bathroom, although from corner to corner it was slightly smaller than my wingspan—good for when you leave your face wash on the sink and need to grab it from the shower, dangerous when you drop the soap.

I didn't have any time to unpack, or any room as the case had been. My roommate had been living by herself for a few weeks and seemed quite comfortable with that arrangement. After I was allowed to drop my bags off, I was escorted to the medical center. I handed them the required medical forms and they whisked me into a back room and administered a flu shot in my arm. A sort of "welcome aboard" from the medical center.

I was then given the necessary emergency instructions that maritime law requires of new employees. Pablo showed me to my emergency station in a way that I would never be able to replicate in an emergency situation. Through vacant hallways, up certain stairways, around luggage carts, I was hoping I could at least remember what floor it was on. Had the ship gone down in the next week I would've been shark bait, not to mention all of the guests I was responsible for in my muster station. I was then shown how to get from my emergency station to the sports deck where I would work and was given a pile of t-shirts—the best uniform on the ship. Next I was taken to the office where I would be responsible for filling out my electronic time sheet, KRONOS. Finally, Pablo handed me a piece of paper to sign saying he had given me extensive directions on what to do in the event of an emergency, to which I responded, "But I have no idea what to do in an emergency situation."

"Yea, I know. I'll tell you that later."

As you may have guessed, this "later" would never come. I was informed of this later through training and other sources, so I felt a little more confident that I would at least survive longer than most of the guests in a crisis. A fact that my mother did not find nearly as comforting as I did.

The next objective on the checklist was to get my formal uniform. Until this point in my life,

I've had the good luck to avoid paying hundreds of dollars for necessary clothes that I'd never wear again—ugly bridesmaid's dresses, balaclavas, that chicken suit that I was able to wear once and swiftly return—but that streak would end today. Details of the attractiveness of the "dress blues" will be discussed later. Thankfully, my everyday work clothes would consist of a Vitality white t-shirt and a royal blue warm up jacket and pants. Finally, I could live out my dream of being able to sleep in my work clothes to save that five extra minutes in the morning if necessary. And necessary it was many-a-night.

Now that we had taken care of formalities, I was hoping there was a nap in my near future, seeing as how I hadn't seen the backs of my eyelids in far longer than I was accustomed to. Maybe I could even unpack, meet my roommate, or eat something that day… the possibilities were endless! That optimism would be crushed shortly, as I was told I had to report for duty at 4:15 p.m., about enough time to change into my uniform and attempt to find my way back to the sports deck.

The rock wall opened to guests at 4:30 p.m. that day, which left Pablo with approximately fifteen minutes to train me. The training consisted of pointing to the conversion chart for shoe sizes, which rarely seemed to be accurate, although I did become excellent at guessing shoe sizes based on accents and height. If guests responded, "9 mate," and they were of the male persuasion, I would hand them our 12.5. It worked out surprisingly well, and when it didn't, we would simply respond, "They're supposed to be tight." Because there was nothing more annoying than trying to tend to four guests at once and having another guest come back and request another shoe size.

After the excellent training in shoe size estimation, I then learned how to harness people. I was shown where we kept the special harnesses that we used for people who we judged to be too small or too large by conventional standards. Next was the challenging harnessing method, which consisted of three main steps: putting the harness around the person's waist, securing it at the belt level, and snapping the straps around each of the legs. Throw a helmet on and send them to the queue. Check.

The last section of my ten-minute rock climbing training was belaying, which I'd never actually done before (for those unfamiliar with rock climbing, belaying is the process of suspending the climber with a rope). The "experience" I'd had with rock walls consisted of fastening carabineers to little kids' harnesses and watching them climb. Granted, I got several birthday party invites while waiting in line with them, but it hadn't exactly prepared me for this.

I should also mention that this was Halloween weekend, which meant there were about 1,000 kids on board this cruise, which also meant the rock wall was swamped and I would have to belay without really having that particular skill set. Luckily the system was essentially fail proof. As long as I hooked the carabineers on the right part of the harness, the automatic brakes would correct any errors I was about to make. This didn't mean that it wouldn't take me an embarrassingly long time to take the tricky carabineers off, or that I wouldn't be yanked in the air when somebody heavier than me was climbing and promptly fell, but I didn't think the "sorry it's my first day" excuse would be very assuring to the guests I was suspending 30 ft in the air.

The first four-hour shift seemed to drag on longer than my journey to Europe. The monotony of belaying what seemed like thousands of people without a break for hours left my shoulders sore and the rest of me exhausted from lack of sleep. But it would still be hours before I was allowed to catch some shuteye.

Instead, I would get to experience the first of my many illustrious parades on the *Voyager*. The parades were quick, but not painless. In order to deliver a successful parade, one needs to swallow their pride and kiss any dignity they may have had goodbye.

The man in charge of parades escorted me to what would be my *Island Frenzy* attire for the next seven months and instructed me to "Just follow the person in front of you and you'll be fine." Fine... that was one way of putting it. I didn't single-handedly destroy the parade, which was my main concern. But there was nothing in my previous 24 years of life that suggested this is where I would end up. Okay, I guess most of the things that had happened in my 24 years of life may have predicted that this is exactly where I would end up, but that doesn't make the blow any less painful.

The entire parade lasted under 10 minutes, and my role consisted of strutting down the promenade in a shimmering sun costume with a rainbow hat, carrying a giant sun on a 10-foot stick, all the while displaying the biggest smile I could muster after not having slept in over 24 hours. Nothing in my mind could comprehend why, but people genuinely seemed to enjoy these parades. Like, adults too. I'm not sure if anybody has ever had the pleasure of witnessing one of these façades first hand, but I challenge you to find some of the videos posted on youTube. Then imagine if you were in it. I bet it will take on an entirely different, more embarrassing meaning.

After my zombie-like performance in the parade (not as an actual zombie though, that would be reserved for tomorrow's Halloween parade), my brain was yearning to see a form of sleep that involved multiple hours strung together in a horizontal position. As I was practically skipping to my beloved bed, I was informed by my Brazilian coworker that drinks after your first parade are mandatory. Fuck.

This is where I would have my first experience with the "back deck," or, the crew bar to all of you landlubbers. While the back deck is like a mini United Nations in that you can hear at least five different languages being spoken at any given time, the most political talk I'd ever heard was regarding which country's soccer team was going to win that night.

The back deck is amazing in its simplicity. The painted murals on the walls gave me a sense of childlike wonderment that brought me back to my days at Spaulding Elementary. Though there were no drawings of worms coming out of apples and slithering toward a book, they did have *very* free-hand drawings of many of the places the *Voyager* stopped, including the Leaning Tower of Pisa and the Coliseum.

The ping-pong table served as a place for me to earn back some of the pride I had lost in the parades, as well as opportunities to win free drinks. It would also serve as the only table big enough to hold the countless amount of cards the BINGO-crazed Filipinos purchased like clockwork every crew BINGO night. There are circular tables small enough to lead you to believe you can pick them up, until you realize they're bolted to the ground, and throw your back out trying. An all-too-often depleted bar in the middle of the room serves as the centerpiece, and lawn chairs, a "DJ booth," and a dance floor make up the rest of the essentials of back deck.

Located at the back of the ship (hence the nickname), it has open-air windows that overlook the wake of a moonlit ocean. I'm not sure if that was for aesthetic purposes or if it was so the bar's patrons wouldn't be inundated with the carbon monoxide poisoning that was sure to result from the thick clouds of cigarette smoke—a staple of the back deck. The open-air windows would also lead to weekly debates regarding whether or not you would be able to sustain a fall, should you get the always-looming urge to jump overboard.

"You'd die on impact."

"No way, it's only like 35 feet."

"You would totally get sucked under the boat."

"Not if you jumped out far enough."

"Well if you survived that the sharks would eat you."

"Most shark attacks are a case of mistaken identity; I think I'd be fine."

"The temperature of the water would kill you in an hour."

"I went swimming in Cape Cod in May, that was pretty cold."

And so on and so forth.

The hands down best feature of back deck was the drink prices. Coming from a college town where dollar drafts of Natural Lite were a bargain, back deck puts even liquor stores to shame. A bottle of Corona ran for $1 on a regular basis. A can of Miller Lite, a mere 85 cents. Top shelf liquors like Jack Daniels and Coke became my drink of choice at a very reasonable $2 a glass, and by glass, I mean red plastic cups that look like they could've been stolen from Pizza Hut. Even better, there was a mandatory gratuity of 18%, which worked out to be a lot less than the $1 per drink standard that American society encourages you to tip. Bartenders on cruise ships also earn their tips much more than most land bartenders I've come across. One shot per drink? You would be hard-pressed to find a ship bartender who believes in *that* policy.

Selling premium drinks nearly at cost when it's in stark violation of the Master's Policies to be drunk on the ship is like preaching an abstinence only policy in school and then handing out free condoms to students after popping in a porn video. What's more is that with little to no daily expenses onboard, your hand is pretty much forced in the matter. Now before you go assuming that I am just another sucker in America's consumer culture, that couldn't be farther from the truth. When it comes to money I consider myself a pretty frugal individual. Sure, I'll splurge for the occasional masterpiece, like a painting of dogs playing poker or a slinky sculpture of my name, but typically the few greenbacks in my wallet rarely see the light of day. I can't even remember the last time I bought something with a respectable brand name. On the ship however, everything is paid for with a crew ID card, a.k.a. monopoly money—a seemingly endless supply of monopoly money—and the itch to purchase something usually manifests itself in buying rounds of drinks between five and seven nights a week.

Three drinks after our 12:30 a.m. arrival to the back deck, and about two and a half drinks more than I wanted, I crawled back to cabin 4256, which I was pretty sure was mine, and met my roommate for the first time.

# CHAPTER VI: GOLD STANDARDS

*Lesson I've learned the hard way #101: Sexual harassment training does little to prevent sexual harassment on cruise ships.*

My roommate, Cynthia, was a 35-year-old dancer from Argentina who I was told spoke little English. Immersion is the best way to learn a language, right? It probably would've been, had both of us ever been awake at the same time. Cruise line dancers tend to have, how do I put this, "jokes" of a schedule. Granted, the job I held on the sports staff was heavily sought after due to its lesser time requirements and relatively laid-back nature, but a dancer's job of appearing in a two-hour long nightly show probably demanded a maximum fifteen hours of work a week. This, in a place where many employees averaged 12-16 hour shifts a day. So when I would be going to work at 6:00 a.m., she would be returning to the cabin to sleep after partying all night at the back deck, understandably letting off steam from such a stressful evening of work. We would exchange a cordial "Buenos días," and I would respond with "Buenas noches," and that was about the extent of our language acquirement.

Cynthia seemed nice enough. She would let me follow her to the mess hall until I finally learned the route myself. She even spoke slightly slower Spanish when I sat at the table with her and her Argentinean friends—though it didn't help much, as she was one of the fastest speakers I've ever heard. Listening to her was like watching Telemundo in fast forward. And while she never asked me to drink yerba mate out of her traditional calabash gourd and *bombilla*—a gesture which in Argentinean culture would have signified that I was welcome and friendly enough to share a communal teacup—that was probably for the best, as a handful of the Argentineans were confined with the flu after indulging in a tea session.

Day number two was fun-filled with a combination of patronizing training and redundant work. As per usual, I needed to wake up hours before Cynthia (about 10 hours to be more precise), and being the considerate roommate I am, I opted not to turn the lights on. Instead, I missed a rung in the bunk ladder and came to a crashing halt on the floor, probably loud enough to wake up our immediate neighbors, but not Cynthia.

After bandaging my wounds up and getting dressed in the dark, it was time for my first of many trainings. These consisted of, among other things, the benefits of showering on a daily basis and changing underwear. I learned that "sexual harassment" means very different things to different people and nudged the creep from Mauritius when the woman training us mentioned, "Guys, if they don't call you back after 15 calls, and say no to all of your questions, they're not interested in you, leave them alone." That's right, it had taken less than a week for me to attract my first scumbag stalker, hell, it had taken less than two hours from the time he had first talked to me to the time I realized he was ready to take me as his bride. After making a conscious effort to avoid him for weeks, he finally latched on to a new host.

We learned the dangers of smuggling narcotics and weapons onboard, the benefits of working in such a diverse environment, more zero-tolerance policies than I can remember, business ethics, sexual ethics, pre-departure safety training, personal survival, crowd management, the ship's "Save the Waves" policy, and my personal favorite, the GOLD standards. G= Greet and smile, O=Own the Problem, L=Look the Part, D=Deliver the Wow. If a new hire new nothing else about the ship after the first week, they knew this. The GOLD standards are the bread and butter of Royal Caribbean's training program. Sure, we devoted all of about ten minutes to going over which of four fire extinguishers to use in different types of fires, not that I remembered any of *that* one hour later, but it seemed like half of the fifteen trainings I had to attend involved beating the GOLD standards into our heads. That and DO NOT SLEEP WITH GUESTS. Evidently a rampant problem on the ships.

The worst part of training wasn't that you had to wake up early on a day that you may have had a morning off, or that the videos were grossly outdated and embarrassingly cheesy, or even that I had learned much of it in 6th grade Health Ed. class. It was the fact they managed to drag out about 8 hours of training over the course of three weeks. A twenty-minute training session in the middle of the day was just enough to prevent one from getting off the ship and enjoying part of the day in the ports—the best part of working on a ship in my opinion. I would've preferred to miss sleep one night and finished the trainings right then and there than to drag it out for 20 days.

There was, however, a little excitement in the first week of training. No, I'm not talking about the shrill chants of "superstar" that the Training & Developing Director was far too fond of, or putting tacks up on a map in order to have a visual of just how diverse the ship was, although my class had a heavy concentration in the Philippines and Peru. No, I'm talking about the first crime I witnessed on the ship. Did somebody get thrown overboard? No. Was a bomb discovered? Not quite. Was a cell phone that was probably misplaced reported as stolen in the training room while we took a bathroom break? It most certainly was.

Kathryn, an Irish girl who often needed a phone call to remind her that she had training (which was odd since the T&D refused to let some people in 2 minutes late) and upon arriving late to training looked like she'd somehow managed to find a truck onboard and heaved herself in front of it, was certain that she had her phone in the training room for the first half of the session. After returning from a five-minute break, she discovered her cellular device had vanished. Now I'm not calling anybody a liar, but if somebody had the balls to steal a phone in the first couple days of joining the ship with cameras allegedly all over the place, they've got to be either really stupid or really poor (probably both in this case).

This allegation required a visit from the *Voyager's* Chief of Security, Mike, to scare the shit out of us. Mike, an intimidating, grumpy, middle-aged Brit, stood about 6'0", but seemed much taller when he was yelling at you. After denigrating the class for 10 minutes, he assured us there would be no consequences if the perpetrator returned the phone to his office by 4 p.m. that day. I was not quite sure what the consequences would be if that didn't happen; after all, Kathryn's cell phone didn't seem a worthy item to search the cameras for, and there was really no other way of finding the person. A fact that the perp must've taken into consideration, because nobody came forward. The mystery of the missing cell phone remains a cold case; perhaps Kathryn will find it in a different pair of pants one of these days, or maybe whoever stole it made more from selling that phone than they will in an entire contract as a dishwasher on Royal Caribbean.

Okay, so a missing cell phone wasn't exactly the kind of excitement I was expecting to find by living on a giant globetrotting ship, but it was my first week, and training was boring enough to make even that interesting. For instance, after the completion of my first week, I found the FAQ page on the Seven Seas Group website to be an entertaining piece of literature. So interesting, in fact, that I felt obliged to share it with you fine people. Below are some of the highlights with both the published answers and my corrected, actual answers in case anybody is considering a career in the cruise industry.

### 1. What is the minimum age requirement to work on a cruise ship?

*The minimum age required to work on a cruise ship is 21.*

*FALSE.* There were plenty of people under the age of twenty-one on the ship, including nineteen-year-old dancers, twenty-year-old spa girls, and one particular girl in the dining room staff who looked to be about twelve, but I will assume was at least eighteen.

### 7. How long does the recruitment process take from start to finish?
*It is hard to determine the length of the recruitment process, but we could estimate that from the moment you register and submit your resume to The Seven Seas Group/SSG Europa, it can take from six to eight months and even longer if the position you are applying for is not open. Of course, it also depends if you are a selected candidate by the cruise line and you have completed your medical tests, visa requirements and Police record check.*

Well, I don't believe I ever actually applied through the Seven Seas Group website, so perhaps it would've taken 6-8 months had I been dealing with them the entire time, but I would estimate it took about one month from the time I posted my resume on some job site, to the time it took Seven Seas Group to ask if I was available for a job interview. Then I had two interviews and a job within the week, and a ship assignment about five weeks after that.

### 9. Are married couples accommodated on the same ship, if hired?

*Although it can be requested, it is never guaranteed that you and your spouse will be scheduled to the same ship.*

This was true unfortunately. Not that it mattered much to me, but I did find the whole "official ship relationship" process odd. From what I understood, you can register as a couple with the crew office, and they will try to put you in a room together, although oftentimes the room would be a regular double, meaning bunk beds. If you got lucky or had been on the ship longer than all of the other couples, you may have had a modified room with one, slightly larger bed, not quite a twin, but not quite a double. If you were dating a staff member or an officer and you were a crewmember, you were still not allowed to eat in the staff and officer mess, but if you were married to a staff member or officer then you were permitted to eat with your spouse. See, they're accommodating! You hear that crew? Marrying a staff or officer will grant you special restricted access to taco night three times a week! If there's a better reason to get married I don't want to know it.

I was also surprised to see how many people have boyfriends/girlfriends or spouses on other ships. How exactly those relationships are considered relationships is beyond me. Not only are you thousands of miles away from your loved one, but something as simple as communicating with anybody is incredibly difficult in the Atlantic, not to mention costly. I know you're not allowed to make requests on your first contract, and RCI is not obliged to honor your requests on any contract thereafter, but is it really that difficult to keep married couples together? Then again, after working in such close quarters for upwards of seven or eight months, maybe Royal Caribbean is indirectly keeping couples together by keeping them apart.

### 12. Do I need a medical test?

*Yes, all cruise lines require a medical test. The Seven Seas Group/SSG Europa may suggest where to go to for a Pre-Employment Medical Examination if available in your town or close by. You may also choose your own certified physician. It is imperative that you pass this medical test before joining the ship and all the results of the test must be presented upon joining a ship. The cost of this examination varies from country to country and is at the expense of the employee.*

FALSE. While I've read in several places how "mandatory" or "imperative" it is that I pass a medical test before joining the ship, it is simply not true. Unless I am to believe I am the one exception to this rule, which, with my arrival, I can't believe is the case, then you can walk right on that ship with nothing more than your letter of employment and a passport. Before I left for Rome, I noticed that my doctor had carelessly ignored an entire section that said I was not blind or deaf (but then again, attention to detail has always been overrated in the medical profession).

And by "before I left for Rome," I mean about an hour before I boarded my flight. After signing my contract, I did drop off my medical papers and was contacted a few days later regarding a hepatitis C test that wasn't done. I was told I would need to get tested for it in Barcelona for €100. Now, I was curious as to why Javier had me send him my medical information if it was not to make sure I had everything completed. Instead, he gave me a supportive, "yes, that all looks good" when I asked him if it was complete. I was also curious as to why my physician, whose time I have taken up about once every three years, missed several portions of the medical tests RCI needed done. Then I remembered. She sucks.

Venting out my frustrations with Dr. Powers wasn't going to help now, however, so I asked if it would be okay if I had the test done when we arrived in Galveston, TX, next month so my insurance would cover it. Obviously, as with every other decision that needed to be made on Royal Caribbean, she needed to consult her superior, which in this instance was human resources for some reason. Scratch that, *I* needed to meet with HR and ask him if he would permit me to postpone the hepatitis C test until we reached American soil.

*If I have any problems with my liver, it's going to be alcohol-related, not hepatitis C*, I thought to myself as I waited anxiously outside HR for my meeting. I pleaded my case to the very understanding Canadian, and he agreed that, "Yeah, you don't look like you have hepatitis C, but you have to get the test done the first chance you get when we get to Texas."

I was grateful that my un-jaundiced appearance allowed me to defer my test to the fine people of Texas and got the medical center off my back for a month. Lucky for him, I left my dirty needles at home.

### 13. Would I get any training?
*Yes, you will be provided with all safety training required by International Maritime laws. Additionally, you can expect to receive training in ethics, corporate culture, service, inter-cultural sensitivity and any training offered by your supervisor or a representative of the training & development department to optimize the efficiency of your job performance, customer service and company standards.*

*TRUE.* As mentioned previously, there was plenty of training that typically begins the day you board the ship, although in my case, my boss called me out of it so I could work. Which is akin to being called out of school to get a root canal done…but then making up that day of school at the end of the year. Thankfully the ship managed to stay afloat the entire time I was there.

### 15. How would I get paid and in what currency?
*Most cruise lines pay their employees twice a month in US Dollars and the wages paid are determined by the cruise line based on the position you have been hired for and the contract you have accepted by signing at the time you join the ship.*

*TRUE.* What they neglect to mention is that they will pay you in the most inefficient and inconvenient way possible. The entire process seemed senseless for a company that has been on the scene since the sixties. I will try to talk you through it here, although you really have to be there to fully grasp the true ridiculousness of RCI's compensation methods.

The phenomenon of payday occurs every other week, with different departments being paid at different times. My department, which consisted of dancers, singers, sports staff, youth staff, broadcast technicians, sound technicians, etc., was deemed worthy of the 7:30-8:15 a.m. time slot. Not the best, but certainly not the worst pay period. Attending your department's pay period in person is mandatory, and when I say mandatory, I don't mean "you must have all of your medical forms filled out to board the ship" mandatory, I mean "the ship's going down and you need to report to your muster station" mandatory. The closer it gets to the end of your pay period time slot, the more frequent the calls to your room become. But as frequently as I contemplated sleeping through payday—nearly every time I wasn't already required to be up for work—I was fortunately never on the other end of one of those phone calls. Sure, part of that was because I wanted my reward for belaying thousands of kids up the rock wall, but the other reason was that the CPA is the one who has to sit there and make sure everybody in our department gets paid, and you do not want to be on the CPA's bad side.

The CPA, or, Cruise Programs Administrator to those of you who may have confused it with the much more popular, and much geekier acronym, is in charge of all of the logistics of the entertainment division, including but not limited to: room assignments, checking attendance at parades, and deciding who gets to "volunteer" to blow up 3,000 balloons for a New Year's Eve party. In short, not one of the best people on the ship to cross—especially at 7:30 in the morning. Ergo, 100% punctual attendance at payday from this girl.

By the time I usually got there at, I don't know, 7:36 a.m., the line was typically wrapped around the door and down the stairs—always encouraging after 4 hours of sleep. After you talk to your line neighbors in an attempt to piece together the previous night's happenings, you've usually waited long enough to make it into the main room which consisted of—and I'm not making this up—the "slop chest." For those of you unfamiliar with maritime terminology, there is a plethora of words that would make one think the entire culture was created by drunken pirates or teenage boys.

These are all actual terms, many of which are still apparently used today: baggywrinkle, blue peter, booby hatch, boy seaman, coxswain, cunt splice, cuntline, deadwood, futtocks, gooseneck, jigger-mast, mess, monkey fist, no room to swing a cat, poop deck, scuttlebutt, seacock, seaman, spanker, spanker-mast, and tailshaft to name a few. All of which I believe I have seen on urbandictionary.com at one point or another. I mean really, a "poop deck" is technically a high deck on the aft superstructure of a ship, but my guess is it was so labeled after Peg Leg Willy didn't have the fortitude to stumble his way back to a bathroom and defecated all over deck 10 of *The Howling Whore*. Poor Willy probably never drank again.

If I may return to the slop chest, which contains such necessities as Milky Way bars and *Most Extreme Challenge Seasons 2 and 3*, it is also the dark, sullen room that holds the thousands of dollars for every crew member's salary on payday. When you're lucky enough to finally enter the slop chest room, the optimism you feel that you are so close to being paid is swiftly crushed when the CPA hands you your bill for the past two weeks. My first bill looked something like this:

> $27.73 High Notes
> $20.00 Portofino's
> $3.00 Portofino's (tips show up separately just to ensure that I always had two pages of bills)
> $10.45 Crew Café (internet)
> $5.90 Johnny Rockets
> $25.20 Crew bar
> $7.65 Crew bar
> $22.15 Vault (the ship's discothèque)
> $7.20 Café Promenade
> $30.50 Uniform Blouse
> $25.00 Uniform Skirt
> $55.00 Uniform warm-up suit
> $14.95 Uniform shorts
> $3.75 Crew bar

$6.83 Crew bar
$1.30 Crew bar
$4.56 Crew café
$5.67 Crew café
$10.94 Crew bar
$2.30 Crew bar
$15.93 Crew bar
Etc.

After receiving this bill, which shows you how much you owe, you wait some more, and then you reach a table with three financial bodies sitting at it. The first person takes your crew ID card and finds the envelope of cash with your name on it. This envelope warns at the top, "Unless you discuss with your manager immediately, this pay slip will show that you received the correct payment of all money owed to you from the employer, vessel owner and Captain." You then have approximately 1.2 seconds to count all of the money down to the penny, before surrendering a good portion of it to the next person at the table to pay your bill. If you take any more than that, the dirty looks and sighs of impatience from the crewmembers behind you are enough to convince you that it's all there and you move along as quickly as possible.

Looking at the pay envelope for the first time I had no idea what number I was actually supposed to be checking. There are all kinds of crazy numbers on those things, some of which weren't even labeled. It was like looking at a weird, unsolvable sudoku...through beer goggles.

Of all the crew operations on the ship that would have me believing that a Royal Caribbean ship was an anomaly of time, perpetually stuck in the dark ages, payday struck me as one of the most asinine. The fact that you must physically pick up your pay in a 45 minute window every other week, the fact that your charges cannot be deducted from your paycheck, the fact that you don't even receive a paycheck but instead are given a wad of cash with no place to deposit it, and the fact that you are paid in hundred dollar bills begs the question, who came up with this method and have they spent any time on the spanker mast for it yet?

In general, seamen are not renowned for their upstanding moral character, and thousands of dollars of cash being stolen from roommates is not unheard of. Why the financial controller would not see it fit to setup direct deposit is beyond me. I posed the question once and was told that it would be too difficult to change over the different currencies. "Ah," I said out loud, while in my head I was thinking, "Don't the banks do that for you?"

Even if they didn't, as an American, with an American bank that always accepts American dollars, would it not be possible for the thirteen or so Americans onboard to setup direct deposit? That could have been our reward for being the only citizens on the ship who were actually made to pay taxes to our native land. You see, Americans are the only employees onboard whose federal tax is taken out every payday, and watching that $850 drop to $800 would have been more bearable with the comforting fact that it would be accumulating a 0.03% interest safe and sound in a bank. Not to mention, having only hundred dollar bills in your wallet makes it considerably more difficult to haggle a lower taxi fare in the Caribbean.

### 19. How can I send money home?
*Sending money home or directly to your bank account is quick and easy. There are many options to send money home whilst onboard, but we recommend the following two: the crew office on most ships offers Crew Wire and money order services. To wire money, you must have all the details of the bank where you want to wire your money to. Both services are offered for a small fee. Inquire at the Crew Office for further details.*

FALSE. Sending money home requires a crew wire sheet that must be filled out prior to boarding if you're hoping to avoid the world's largest headache. The crew office requires that you get a print out from your bank detailing your account number, address of the bank, routing number, etc. In order to do this however, you would need to walk across the ship to the internet, try to find a computer that wasn't occupied or broken (good luck), avoid passing out in the blazing heat that often saturated the room, find the various requirements and print them all out.

However, I was not made aware of the fact that there was even a printer in the Internet room until my last week onboard. One would think when I asked the financial controller how I could accomplish a seemingly trivial task anywhere else in the world, he would have told me this tidbit of information. Instead, he told me to "talk to my supervisor," the inevitable answer to any questions any employee might ever have onboard. Surely your supervisor would tell you about a printer in the Internet room right? That would've made the most sense, but the *Voyager* was never about doing things that make the most sense. "Email me the information and I will print it out for you," Pablo told me. Another trip across the ship to wait for a computer. After twenty minutes of waiting for a computer with nothing to do but scour through the crew library, which contained such classics as *Filipino Earth Tales* and every Danielle Steele book ever written, somebody had the decency to wrap up their hour and a half internet session. He did not however, have the same decency to close out of his "www.latinabrides.com" webpage, but I wish him and Maria del Carmen the best of luck in their future matrimony—a true match made in heaven. After swiping my crew card, I emailed all of the information that was needed to my noble supervisor. He printed it out days later, at which point I sought out the financial controller again. Lunch break. By the time he would come back I would have to be at work. I'll try tomorrow.

I finally timed my day to coincide with his open hours, albeit skipping my only opportunity to eat lunch that day, and was informed that I was missing the address of the bank on the print out. The computer must've cut if off when Pablo printed it out. Fantastic. "Well I wrote it down here I'm 100% sure that's correct, and you have the bank's routing number print out right here, which should really be all you need right?" Praying that he would choose to use those critical thinking skills I'm sure everybody over the age of 18 is capable of, I waited in anticipation of the disappointing answer I already knew was coming. "No, there is a space for address on this crew wire, it must all be filled out." At this point, I decided that it would be safer to keep thousands of dollars of cash unlocked in my cabin than to entrust it to the Royal Caribbean financial office.

**20. What would be the nationality of the contract that I will be signing upon joining the ship?**
*In most cases the contract issued by a cruise line is a contract written and issued to the crewmember in accordance to International Maritime Laws; however, there may be cases where the crewmember's contract may be attached to the specific flag of the ship or the country to which the cruise line operates from.*

WTF? I can't imagine that this question gets asked enough to label it a "Frequently Asked Question." In fact, I can't imagine most of the people who sign up for a job on a cruise ship are the least bit concerned with the nationality of the contract that they will be signing, but after reading the answer to a question that I never would've considered asking, I am now more confused and concerned that I *should* care about what nationality my contract is written under. But it's good to know that sometimes it is issued in accordance to International Maritime Laws, and sometimes it's not. Duly noted.

## 21. Who pays for my flight to the ship and back home?

*All travel expenses to join the ship will be at the expense of the new employee. On the contrary, your airline ticket to return home will be paid by the cruise line only when the contract length has been fulfilled.*

*FALSE.* This knowledge proved to be wrong on both accounts. While I don't want to repeat myself or give away the dramatic ending to the book, I neither paid for my flight over to Rome (they never ended up taking it out of my pay, although I'm sure this was unintentional), nor did I have to pay for my flight when my contract length had not been fulfilled. Deedee: 2 Royal Caribbean: 0.

## 22. Do I need to buy any uniforms?

*Most positions onboard cruise ships will require you to wear a uniform and either the entire uniform or part it may be at your expense. If your position requires you to pay for the uniform or part of it, you will be charged through your onboard account, which you are responsible for and must ensure it is kept current by settling it at the end of each payroll period.*

*TRUE*—Unfortunately. However, what they neglect to mention is that some of the uniforms are so hideous that they hope you will leave it in the lost and found of the ship so that you don't have to waste precious space in your luggage that could otherwise be taken up by the

Nacho Libre masks or cheap tequila that Mexico makes look so enticing. At least this is where I'm fairly certain my ill-fitting blouse came from, as there was loose thread and broken cufflink buttons after the first time I wore it. Another piece of the infamous "dress blues," whose aim it seemed, was to make us look like uglier versions of Julie from *The Love Boat,* was a navy blue blazer (also broke a cufflink button the first time I wore it), a khaki skirt, which more accurately resembled a brown paper grocery bag than something one would voluntarily don as apparel (then again I guess nobody did voluntarily wear them). The shoes were black, closed-toe heels, worn to ensure that in the slim possibility that some people fancied the uniform, at least nobody would match.

After the first two weeks of wearing my dress blues, a passing stranger in the hallway mentioned to me, "You know we have a tailor on the ship, right?"

"Why no sir, I didn't, but it was nice to meet you too."

And so back I went to my supervisor, the only person that is obligated by contract to answer my questions. While I wanted to ask him why he saw me wearing an oversized bag as a uniform and opted not to disclose information of a tailor, I had slowly become impervious to the fact that things were not taught on the ship but learned, often the hard way. Hence, I asked him solely for directions to the tailor and if he knew the hours of operation.

"It's near where you got your uniform, I don't know the hours, you'll have to check," he responded with the same stone-cold face and annoyed tone that he answered all of my seemingly obvious questions with. Did I have the slightest clue as to where in the massive ship he had led me to get my uniform within an hour of boarding that first day? Of course not. I had been traveling for what seemed like days, jet lagged in the worst sense of the word, still trying determine if I had just made the biggest mistake of my life, and I was essentially led by the hand through a labyrinth of featureless hallways and staircases to a caged "office" which held all of the treasured uniforms of Royal Caribbean. Assuming that, like nearly every other entity on the ship, the tailor would only be open during hours that I had to work, lunch would have to wait for another day again.

I worked on the aft of the fourteenth floor, which aside from the one room Chapel above us, was the top of the ship. The tailor, word had it, was in the front of the Tween Deck, two floors below "Deck 1" and well below any rooms that had a chance of seeing sunlight. In other words, the two points on the ship farthest from each other. Luckily, that beautiful invention I like to refer to as "the elevator" has been known cut travel time on ships exponentially. Or so it would have, had we not stopped on nine of the ten floors I rode it for. I never could quite grasp the concept of waiting five minutes for an elevator to bring you down one floor. If I cannot see any immediate evidence of a broken leg or a hospital stretcher, then I reserve the right to stare daggers through you for abusing such technology. I digress.

After making it to the Tween Deck and being blasted with a wave of heat, combined with a tinge of body odor, and a whole lot of confused Filipino faces, I had arrived in the laundry room. Once we got past the language barrier,[7] I sprinted through the watertight doors, whose force when closed were powerful enough to snap a cow's leg bone as demonstrated in training (why there was a cow's leg bone onboard is one of those bizarre ship questions that you just learn to accept), past dirty linen that was beyond repair, and reached a dead end. I turned around to see what looked like a game of "hot or cold" being played by the laundry crew and would not have been half as frustrated if they had thought to include me in the game with directional advice in the form of varying degrees of temperature. Upon making eye contact, one of the men pointed to a room, which was a solid six paces away from where I began my original journey. There, I had seen what the men were talking about the first time I passed it—it was simply a smaller cage attached to the larger cage of uniforms that I took to be a storage room.

Why hadn't the tailor said something to me as I passed with skirt in hand you may ask? Because there was no tailor anywhere to be seen. Today was a Wednesday, and why would I have the audacity to assume that the small cage would be open on a Wednesday afternoon? Got it, Wednesdays were off days for tailors, as were Thursdays, Saturdays, Sundays, and Mondays.

---

[7] "Sastre" is Tagalog for tailor, apparently.

Another failed trip to the bowels of the ship. I would make another attempt on Friday.

When I finally confirmed the existence of the tailor, she greeted me with "Oh, thank God you come here! I thought you was Amish," in a heavy Jamaican accent. As amused as anybody, I asked her if there was a place I could change, perhaps another side cage, to which she assured me that trying the skirt on would not be necessary. Now, I'm no expert in the field of clothing alteration, but I have had a dress or two hemmed in my day, and I was fairly certain that trying the clothing on was a prerequisite to fitting it to one's body. I guess an alternative method *could* involve holding the skirt up to my waist and asking me how high above the knee I wanted it to sit. She took out a ruler, measured the inch differential and told me to pick it up in three days. Surely she wasn't assuming that the skirt would be the same length with an actual human body inside it, was she?

You know what they say about assuming, it makes an ass out of you and me, mostly me as the case would be, as I had to wear what now looked like one of my botched home economics projects in fifth grade. The handiwork of the seamstress all made perfect sense in one climactic, one-sided shouting match at what would have otherwise been an uneventful boat drill one morning.

I asked if she would care to give it another shot since I was told it was free to get uniforms tailored, to which she fired back, "Well it's not free, you're supposed to tip! It's a side job that I rely on tips for! I just didn't make a big deal of it because I thought you were Amish!" Out of the corner of my eye I could see the emergency raft leader getting ready to tackle one of us, hopefully her, as well as emergency stations 30 A, B, C, and D enjoying the show thoroughly. "I'm sorry," I told her once I picked my jaw up from the ground, but what I was really thinking was "tipping you for something I could've done better myself with a cheap sewing kit and bottle of Jack Daniels would be like tipping a waiter who turned my filet mignon into a hamburger!"

Had she not made such a big deal out of it I would have tipped her, because I'm sure she was on the lower end of the Royal Caribbean pay scale (which was probably less than most people in the first world pay in taxes in any given year), but now it was a matter of principle. Nobody embarrasses me in front of my emergency leader and gets a $3 tip out of it! No, instead I would stick to my standard protocol for such awkward ship situations: ask people when her contract was up and conveniently avoid her on the ship until then.

### 23. How would I clean my uniforms and personal clothing?
*All cruise ships have a laundry facility onboard and uniforms are usually cleaned at no cost to the crewmember; however, you may be charged for personal clothing, including pieces of the uniform without a company logo. Also, most ships today have a crew laundry where you may have access*

*to washing and drying machines available as a self-service (a small fee may apply).*

This was true in the way that Willy Wonka's golden tickets were available to those who wanted them. The laundry crew usually seemed to have their hands full with the thousands of towels and linens the ship went through on any given day, so I tried not to add to their pile of work. Besides, it took three days for them to return your uniforms and I was sitting pretty with only one pair of uniform pants. And so my experience with the laundry was nearly always with the staff laundry.

There were—count 'em—two washers and two dryers for the entire staff of hundreds to use in their free time. And it seemed like everybody on the ship had the same free time as me. Although I admit, if I wanted to stay in the dank first floor of the ship instead of venturing out to the French Riviera while we were docked, I probably would not have had as much difficulty finding an open washer. There were a few additional washing machines available to all of the staff *and* crew, but there was indeed a small fee that applied, and I have principles against paying for things you can get for free, like water, pens, and calendars. Clearly my time was not worth $1.25 a load. So I would play the waiting game in the 8x4ft, 100-degree laundry room nearly once a week. When I reflect back on the ship laundry—as I do so often in my post contract days—one particular anecdote comes to mind that seems to epitomize the entire experience.

It was a beautiful day in Cozumel, Mexico, the type of weather that makes you want to stay on the beach and forget about needing a source of income to survive. As per usual, I had waited until the last possible minute to do laundry, and I don't just mean I had no clean underwear. I've gone to work in my bathing suit bottoms on more than one occasion; I mean I literally did not have any uniform shirts that had not been buried in my hamper for days. So being the responsible, professional sports staffer that I was, I polished off my fish bowl margarita and dragged myself away from sunny paradise to go through that tedious process of washing clothes once again.

Thinking that the weather would attract people outside and leave at least one of the washer's open was clearly a miscalculation. I passed the time that remained on the occupied washer by completing every sudoku I could rummage out of the cruise staff office. The woman whose clothes had just finished—let's call her devil woman—was in the process of removing them as I stood anxiously behind her ready to throw my load in when she reaches into another hamper and throws another load in the washer.

"YOU CAN'T DO THAT!" I wanted to scream at her, trying to uphold some sort of laundry etiquette integrity, but I was too taken aback to do anything other than stare in disbelief. Either waiting there with a bag of dirty laundry and a twitch in my eye did not faze her at all, or she was well versed in this type of trickery and had learned to silence that little courtesy button in her head, that most of us are taught to listen to at a young age.

Fair enough, I thought to myself, by now there was only another 20 minutes left on the other washer, and there was a particularly difficult sudoku that I had not finished. So I waited again, in the windowless, boiling laundry room for the only other washer. Fortunately for me, this person was not as punctual as devil woman, and I wasted no time throwing their clothes on the nearby ironing board and placing mine in the environment they've needed so desperately for the past six days. I returned to my room, all the while doing the math in my head to see if my laundry would be done by the time I had to head up to the sports deck. Forty minutes in the washer, plus forty-five minutes in the dryer, should leave me with approximately twenty-five minutes to shower and eat before work. But this wasn't taking into consideration the fact that the ship gods hated me, and almost everybody else who works on the ship—but especially me.

I returned two minutes early to fend off people from tearing apart my clothes in an effort to claim the washer and couldn't help but notice there was still thirty minutes on devil woman's dryer.

"How is that possible?" I thought to myself. I physically watched her place her clothes in the dryer over forty minutes ago. Then Peter, who had been in the laundry room when most of this laundry shadiness had taken place, opens the dryer and feels devil woman's clothes. Bone dry.

Now I'm not sure who this woman is, or why she feels the need to wash and dry her clothes twice in one session, but it is probably one of the most absurd actions I've ever witnessed in person. It drew all kinds of questions to my mind. Does she do this every time? Does she have some sort of glandular problem that makes sweat stains impossible to remove with one typical wash cycle? How can she possibly spend so long doing laundry and not go crazy? I did not understand.

What I did understand, was that I would never make it to work on time had I waited for her already dry clothes to be cremated. With the encouragement and blessing of Peter, I took her clothes out of the dryer and placed mine in. I took another thirty-minute nap in my luxurious bottom bunk (Cynthia had left two weeks after I arrived, giving me the opportunity to seize the much coveted bottom bunk) and returned to my personal hell for that day. It was at this point I realized my clothes were certainly not in the dryer I put them in. I looked all around the room, which took all of 5 seconds, and realized they were nowhere to be seen. Shit. That was literally all of the clothes I had for the nearly seven months I was to be there, including my work uniforms. It wasn't until another fifteen minutes had passed that I realized devil woman had taken my wet clothes out of the dryer and placed them back in the washer. I was too dumbfounded to call her all the names that were coming to my head at the moment. This was not the 12-year-old looking girl who I had mentioned earlier. Devil woman was at least thirty with the maturity level of an eight-year-old boy and the bitch factor of a teenage girl.

You see, the washer doors lock so that a load cannot be taken out until the cycle is completed. I ripped my sobbing wet clothes out of the washer and ran back to my room. In an act of desperation, I used my roommate's blow dryer to try and dry my work uniform, which consisted of a white cotton t-shirt among other things. As you can imagine, the blow dryer idea failed miserably and thinking the wet t-shirt contest would be less than professional, I was forced to wear my jacket in 90-degree weather. It's a weird sensation wearing a drenched shirt while sweating profusely. Those of you who have not been fortunate enough to experience it should definitely give it a try...I would however, recommend a place other than work to test it out.

### 25. How long is a working day on the ship?
*You can expect to work at least 70 hours per week or as specified in your contract with the cruise line. You may also be asked to work overtime and if it applies to your position, you will be compensated for all hours worked beyond the required hours stipulated per your contract.*

If any of these FAQs encouraged me to run for the hills and never look back it was this one. SEVENTY HOURS A WEEK?! Shit, seventy hours a *month* still seemed like a lot to me. And those two little words "at least" weren't very comforting either. I knew people who worked "at least 70 hours a week." They were called doctors and they made a hell of a lot more than $1700 a month. What would be the point of working on a cruise ship if I would actually be working the entire time? That would be like working in the call center at a Disney World. Unlike a sizeable portion of the crewmembers, I was not going to get rich working here. That kind of money doesn't translate into the millions in my home currency. I was primarily doing it for the experience, to meet to a diversity of fun people, and to travel the world on somebody else's dime, you know, what anybody would want from their employer.

When I voiced my concerns regarding the workload to Javier, he reassured me that that number was the average for all the crewmembers and that I would "most likely" not be working that many hours. What I assumed he meant by this was that the cooks, dishwashers, laundry, and deckhands were the unfortunate souls who would be driving this average up. Sports staff, I would come to find out, drags the average significantly down and has one of the best schedules one can have without boasting any nautical qualifications or ownership of the vessel. This was a particular relief after noticing that the overtime in my contract was set at 303 hours per month. That means that I would have to work 303 hours just to get bumped up to a rate of approximately $8.40 an hour. Otherwise known as the starting rate as a shift leader at the local Taco Bell. Again, I cannot personally complain about working too often in comparison to nearly everybody else on the ship. Of course we took every opportunity to denigrate the few groups that worked less than us (i.e. the ice and dance cast and the musicians), such is human nature after all. Truth be told, the sports staff on our ship managed to elude many of the trivial jobs doled out to our colleagues in the entertainment division, including but not limited to (never limited to): working at the immigration tables upon arriving in America, welcoming people back onto the ship on a port day, or, and this is my favorite, working security.

Typically, one would hope that the ship's security lay in the hands of trained professionals who have at least received basic training in the fundamentals of security operations. And I suppose they have, depending upon whose definition of "basic" you use. I would often return to the ship after a day in Costa Maya or Cozumel, and come to find a youth staffer or a dishwasher, or a bartender swiping guests' ship ID cards and making sure their picture matched their face. Granted, I'm not sure how much training you could give for such a menial task, but I do know if I was a youth staffer who had just worked seven hours and had another five hours to work that night, I certainly wouldn't be putting forth my best efforts to do somebody else's job. Especially with the knowledge that I was not getting paid extra for it. One of my youth staff friends did manage to get a grenade on the ship when she was asked to by the Chief of Security in a test to see just how competent his team was. She hid it in the all too popular place of her backpack, sent it through the x-ray, and boarded the ship seamlessly. She then turned to the Chief of Security to kindly return his explosive. Hopefully things have improved since then.

There were a few opportunities for employees to earn extra money with a part time job, assuming the job you were hired for granted such luxurious amounts of time. Namely, if you were in the dance or ice cast. Examples of some of the part time jobs included working at the art auctions, signing people up for the Crown Anchor Society, and of course, security. As a matter of fact, two members of the dance cast were hired as "extra" security during times with high guest counts to ensure the protection of the ship and its patrons. Because nothing screams "safety and security" more than teenage dancers. Ironically enough, both of them were fired a few months later for excessive alcohol consumption.

Now there were instances where the sports staff attempted to close the gap of the disparate hours worked. When there were high counts of elderly guests, we were part of the coalition to wheel them all up what-didn't-seem-steep-until-you-are-pushing-a-two-hundred-plus-pound-person-up-it-in-a-wheelchair ramp. Royal Caribbean was even kind enough to supply some of us with back braces. I was not one of those fortunate souls. More disparaging was when we were summoned to aid in the decorating of the entire ship for every holiday, from Halloween to Valentine's day, including a fun effort to blow up 3,000 balloons for New Year's which left my fingers nearly paralyzed for hours and the rest of my body in some sort of acid-base imbalance. There was also promenade duty, which consisted of informing people that they were indeed on the promenade in case they were confused or lost. There were tour loads, in which we would walk guests downstairs and point to the bus they need to get onto if they couldn't figure out how to read the sign "ATV through the Mayan Ruins" by themselves. And then there was debarkation, which involved leading guests off the ship in hopes that the next batch would be able to figure this out on their own. All seemed pretty futile to me—especially since they all began before 7 a.m.—but perhaps I'm overestimating the amount of brainpower people wish to exercise while on vacation (after all there were more people signed up for the "Dune Buggy Jungle and Beach Safari Tour" than there were for the Mayan Ruins).

But the youth staff was by our sides for nearly all of those events. They even had the good fortune to sing Christmas Carols with us in the promenade, even though half of them hadn't ever heard the songs before. So I was curious as to why we on the sports staff weren't made to work security at the gates like so many others. Then came my answer.

Turns out, it was *not* standard protocol to grossly inflate your working hours on your KRONOS. Sure I had sat through the business ethics video in training, and I like to think that my moral compass typically points north, but my supervisor, the man in charge of directing, guiding, and informing me during my tenure on the *Voyager*, made himself quite clear on our approach to KRONOS. We needed to exaggerate our hours on a daily basis so they would not reduce the already small sports staff. We needed to write that we worked at some point in the morning, preferably for a couple of hours, and in the evening on port days, totaling at least seven hours, eight or nine on sea days. I was told, "If they don't think we're working as much as these other groups they will cut positions, and since you have the least experience it would be you," or something to that effect. Nothing says, "welcome aboard!" to a new employee like being coerced into cheating your new employer to save your job. It may have been that I half believed Pablo, or it may have been that I thought I could place the blame on him if caught, you know, one of those "just following orders" excuses that have typically never worked in history, but I listened to him. Even if I did want to do the "ethical" thing and report him, I would have had to ask him for directions to Human Resources to do so.

So, as so many do, I took the easy way out. And I didn't have difficulty sleeping at night either. I wasn't siphoning money from UNICEF's emergency fund; this was a billion dollar corporation whose last priority seemed to be its employees. You wouldn't condemn Robin Hood for stealing from the rich and giving to the poor would you? Alright, maybe if you're a Republican or royalty you would, in which case you folks can skip to the next section. But seriously, I cannot think of any other job in which humans are expected to work up to ten months without a single day off. A "day off" in the cruise industry means that you don't have to go into work until 4 p.m. Recognition for all your hard work comes in the form of 77 cent champagne bottles at crew parties, and if you're lucky enough to be one of the two employees of the month, you are awarded a spin on the prize wheel. Prizes ranged from airline flights to Playstations, although every spin I saw landed closer to the "Meal for Two at Johnny Rockets" prize.

In short, a "typical" working day on the ship does not exist. Depending on your job, it can range from two hours to eighteen, and rarely, if ever, is one granted a day off. But alas, that is the uncertainty you sign up for when seeking employment with a cruise ship. You learn to embrace it...or tolerate it at least.

### 26. Would I be allowed to visit Guest areas onboard the ship?

*You may not be allowed in guest areas unless it is to perform a work-related duty. However, some positions may allow you to visit guest's areas whilst off duty as long you are wearing a uniform or the attire required for the day/evening. Either way, keep in mind that guests will always have a first priority anywhere onboard the ship.*

TRUE. You only had to be on the ship for about five minutes before you realize how true the last part of that FAQ is. I've only dreamed of working at a place where employees are given preferential treatment, but sadly that is a pipe dream that would not be realized here.

Fortunately my position granted me the right to venture into guest areas, nametag and dress code permitting. Certain days we had to wear dress blues, long dresses and tuxedos were necessitated on formal nights, and the last day of the cruise mandated all black be worn. Wearing a nametag in guest areas while not on duty posed problems on more than one occasion for my colleagues and myself. Trying to shop for a camera or watch in any of the various shops always took twice as long as expected due to the dozens of questions we would have to field about whether senior citizens received a discount on Royal Caribbean key chains, or if there was any kind of a warrantee on a snow globe.

"I'm sorry I don't work here," my friends and I would respond.

"Well you have a nametag on and you're dressed up."

"Yes, I can understand your confusion as to why you may think I work here, but I can assure you I do not."

"Yeah I recognize you from the rock wall, did anybody beat my time at the speed climb?"

"Only Spiderman sir." This always elicited a chuckle from the older group believe it or not.

"Well good. I don't understand why you're working down here if you work at the rock wall, they kind of seem unrelated to me."

"I'm not working down here, I was just helping my friend pick out a watch."

"Ohhhh, I get it. So you don't know if there's a sale today?"

And so would go several conversations that would result from wearing these scarlet letters throughout guest areas. I typically didn't mind them, despite what the rest of this book may lead you to believe. I do like to meet and talk to new people (a concept that my British sport staff coworker could not fathom), but sometimes the attention would run its course. It was sort of like receiving the negative aspects of being a celebrity (the questions, the interest in our lifestyles, etc.) without the money or prestige to make it worthwhile.

The nametag debacle reached a fever pitch about halfway through my time on the *Voyager*. Up until then, the gym was the only guest area where we were not required to wear our nametags. Then it happened. At one of our oh-so-enlightening divisional meetings we were delivered the horrific news that all employees would be required to wear their name badges to the fitness center. That was it. The last refuge on the ship where we could feel like real human beings for an hour or two. Gone faster than our dignity in the first parade. Of course the uproar over the nametags wasn't just due to the added ounce of weight we would have to bare while running (alright maybe that wasn't anybody else's concern), but the issue of having to work when we weren't on duty. It didn't matter if I was wearing a zebra print leotard, listening to my iPod while watching TV on a treadmill, if guests saw that name tag they would ask you all kinds of questions. How does this machine work? Do you think it's better to do push ups or bicep curls to get definition? What are the hours you can get a personal trainer? What's your blood type? Okay, that last question was never posed to me personally, but you get the idea.

I can recall one instance where I was running on the treadmill with headphones in my ears and a guest tapped me on the arm.

"Excuse me, could you show me how this leg press machine works?"

After turning off my iPod and stopping my treadmill I addressed the elderly lady, "Oh I don't work here but that man over there can help you," pointing to a fitness instructor.

"Yes you do, I see your nametag, that's why I came up to you."

*Well thank God for these nametags*, I thought to myself. Instead of arguing with the guest, I left my machine to walk her through it. Partly because she had clearly looked at my name and I didn't want her to leave a bad comment about me, but mostly because she bore a striking resemblance to Betty White and I simply could not say no to her. I showed her how the machine worked and she attempted to execute the motion.

"It's too heavy I can't do it."

It was set for 20 lbs. Newborns can lift 20 lbs with their legs.

"You may need to adjust the weight."

"How do I do that?"

"Just pull that pin out and put it...on second thought, just pull the pin out."

At this point she was lifting the weight of the leg lift, about three pounds by my estimate. But more importantly she was occupied. I bid her farewell and any motivation I once had to return to the treadmill while the boat was careening back and forth was lost. I really hated these nametags.

Another reason I grew to despise these nametags was because it left a terrible rash on my skin that I hadn't experienced since before my mom started to splurge on baby powder. Let me clarify. There are two different types of metal nametags Royal Caribbean carries. One, the first one I was given, had a magnet on the back so you didn't have to put holes through your clothes every time you affixed it to your uniform. I had never seen a magnetized nametag before (I assume it's a good thing that my prior jobs have not educated me on the wide array of various nametags) and thought it was a great idea. It prevented ripping your clothes, it was easy to put on, and it was fun to knock off of your coworkers whenever you wanted. Then there was the other option for identifying employees.

The standard nametag has that annoying little pin that takes much longer to put on, and can't be knocked off at all without tearing apart your clothing. And, as I would come to find out, is made with a type of metal that I am clearly and unfortunately allergic to.

Of course, I never would have found this out had it not been for one day in the Internet room. As per usual, the room was smoldering. I'm not sure if this was a strategic move to keep times on the computer down, if the thermostat was broken, or if the ship's IT guys thought computers had to be kept in 80 degree weather so as not to spoil. You know, like a greenhouse for PCs. Whatever it was, it had caused me to take my uniform jacket off with my cool magnetic nametag on it. After sending out emails and posting "Happy birthdays" on my friends' facebook walls, I got out of there before beads of sweat accumulated all over my body, forgetting to grab my jacket on my expedited exit.

When I realized my mistake thirty minutes later, I headed back to the chair I had left my coat on only to discover it was nowhere to be seen. Nobody in the room claimed to have seen it, although I had heard those swanky blue jackets were a hot commodity on the ship. Why crew and staff members could not simply buy them from the uniform department like everybody in the sport and youth staff had to is beyond me. Perhaps they were considered one of the benefits of the job, because God knows the healthcare didn't qualify as one of those. Surprisingly, nobody had turned my jacket WITH NAMETAG in to security, and security certainly did not care, they had bigger problems with their grenade-sniffing department anyway.

Since I had to work in an hour, I walked over to the office to get a new nametag.

"Hey, Daniel, My jacket was stolen and it had my nametag on it, could I get another one?" I mention the part about my jacket being stolen because there is typically a $5 charge for a new nametag. However, given my current situation, Daniel takes pity on me and waves the fee—a true hero. His chivalry would lose some of its luster when I noticed many of the stuffed animals on the front desk have nametags like "Banana Bob" on the gorilla or "Teddy" on the bear (clever right?).

As Daniel hands me my shiny new nametag I can't help but notice there is no magnet on it.

"Oh hey, Daniel would it be possible to get one with a magnet by chance?" Trying not to push my luck.

"We're out of those right now, check back next week."

Damn you, Banana Bob! Alright fine, I can deal with the lame nametag for a week I guess, who cares if it looks like I had an acupuncture session with my shirt on? Not me. What did bother me however, was the tiny, itchy red bumps that began to develop in the upper left quadrant of my chest where I would typically don my nametag.

"Hmm…that's odd," I thought, as I inspected the metal to make sure there was no hepatitis C lurking on it (I assume that's possible?). The needle looked clean enough, but it was still responsible for an increasingly large blemish on my skin that was not particularly attractive in a bathing suit. I ruled out the idea that this was an act of karma, retaliating at me for all those wise cracks I had made at a youth staffer's expense regarding her leprosy-like hives she had acquired from a day in Mexico, and returned to the office a week later to see if the new shipment of magnets had arrived.

My answer would come in the form of every other question I had on the ship: disappointment. "No, we didn't get any magnets yet Deedee, check back next week."

"Are you sure there are magnets coming next week?" I asked with all the hope of a child begging Santa for a new easy bake oven, except in my case, skin cream would have been more practical.

"They should be."

Should be. I knew what "should be" meant. It meant an irrevocable "no." Just like the time I asked my friend if there were new batteries in my calculator I let him borrow right before I took the SAT II and it died on me. Just like the time I asked if my friend's dog was potty-trained right before she relieved herself all over my room. Just like the time I asked if a black diamond trail at Jiminy Peak had recently been groomed when I was eight years old and just learning to ski.

I checked back with Daniel multiple times a week for three and a half weeks, all the while trying to suppress the red monster that was spreading like a wildfire on my chest with hydrocortisone cream: unsuccessfully, I may add. Then one day I showed up for work and Jason, my British coworker appears with a brand new magnetic nametag. How did I know it was new you might ask? Because Jason, who has never attempted to learn, never even shown interest in learning a language other than English, had a Spanish flag on his nametag, indicating that he is fluent in that language.

"Hey uh, Jason? Where the hell did you get that nametag?" I asked him.

"Oh yea, right, the crew office gave it to me. Riley dared me to chuck mine overboard and yell 'I QUIIIITTT!!!' last night at the back deck, so I did."

After about three minutes, my laughter turned to confusion, and then rage.

"How were you able to get one with the magnet?"

"Daniel gave it to me."

"That son of a bitch…he told me they were out of them!"

"Yeah I think I got the last one."

Well that's fucking fantastic. I've been trying to get my hands on one of those for nearly a month after mine was stolen, and Jason launches his overboard while hammered and gets one within a few hours. This also leads me to believe karma is not involved.

"So I take it they don't test you on your language fluency before throwing those flags on your badge?"

"Ha, not at all. I actually told him to put the Japanese flag on it, but he said they didn't have any. So I told him to just throw a Spanish flag on there, to which he replied, 'Wow you speak three languages? Good for you!'"

"Yeah I know, I'm awesome," Jason retorted to Daniel.

"And humble," I replied to his retelling of the story.

Once I was relieved from my duties of work, I headed straight to the office, which in my fury I had forgotten would not be open until tomorrow.

"Daniel! Did you give away a magnet nametag!?" I asked/shouted.

"Yes, Jason needed one and the front desk wanted to make Banana Bob trilingual so I had to make him a new one."

At this point I just close my eyes and sigh, knowing full well that this should've been expected. Why would I *not* expect Banana Bob to be trilingual? After all, he was a sharp dresser, he worked at the front desk, and he seemed educated enough. His nametag should reflect this.

Once all of the stuffed animals and people who had voluntarily tossed their nametags to the sharks were fully equipped with nametags that didn't result in rashes, I was finally granted one. And you better believe that I had them throw the Spanish flag on that bitch.

### 34. Are there any prospects for career advancement?

*Cruise Lines often offer training courses you can take advantage of that will help you advance in your career at sea. Also, cross-training programs may also be available which will be a step forward to a promotion. Opportunities on cruise ships are extensive, but it all depends on you and what direction you would like to take your shipboard career.*

Translation: if you can play by their rules and tolerate ship life for more than two years you will be promoted. My personal observation on the ship would seem to indicate that seniority outweighs competence in supervisor positions in nearly every department. Just what you would hope to find in any organization. Sarah may not know how to adjust the sound levels in the studio, but she hasn't pissed anybody off in two years, let's promote her. This seemed to be the logic that had launched so many of the supervisors into their illustrious careers.

Of course, this promotion took a little longer for employees from the Philippines and India. I was talking to one of the Indian cleaners who told me that his recruiting office told him that even though his $500 a month "salary", if you could call it that, looked low for 14 hours of backbreaking labor a day, he would be promoted to manager within a few months. Once he signed the contract and arrived on the ship however, he learned the sad truth of which all of his predecessors were now aware. Like a tourist who buys that dirt-cheap iPhone on the streets of Paris only to realize later that it's just a nicely painted rock, Putra could no longer do anything about his situation once he was onboard. He couldn't afford a plane ticket home; he had quit his job at home for the promise of a better salary and had a wife and kids to support.

"What are you going to do?" I asked him.

"What can I do? I must work."

I wanted to ask him if there was an organization he could appeal to in India, but thinking better of it I exchanged a sympathetic look with him.

"Is there anything Royal Caribbean can do about it?"

After he stopped laughing he responded with, "Of course there's something they *could* do, but then they wouldn't have half of their workers from India. This is what most of my paisanos are told, and then we get here and find out what it's really like, but what can we do at this point?"

I couldn't help but draw parallels from my conversation with Putra and one of my classes in which we discussed sex trafficking. All too often women and children from underprivileged backgrounds are lured into a different country with the promise of a better job that pays more than they would be able to make at home. Once they have been removed from everything and everybody they know, and with little resources available to them, they often find themselves stuck in a situation that they cannot get out of. Of course sex trafficking often involves the use of violence and drugs to retain power over its victims, but I said parallels, not a perfect fit. It seems unlikely that Royal Caribbean is completely ignorant to this form of deception. Much like the businessman buying a stereo out of some man's van in a dark alley for a discount price, the fact that they get their product for a cheap price is all that matters in their eyes. The ends justify the means. The fact that Royal Caribbean allows this deception to happen continues to chip away at their integrity.

But then again, it's not only the under-educated and impoverished employees from the developing world who are misled in the recruitment process utilized by Royal Caribbean, and, I'm all too certain, its competitors. Hell, this entire chapter has been a broad example of how misrepresentative, if not straight out false, the information given to prospective employees is. Apparently, even an American with two higher degrees can believe the hype. The truth is, no one, myself included, knows a damn thing about what they are getting into until they already have their sea legs, and the life (and port) that they disembarked from is too far gone to turn back.

# CHAPTER VII: FLAGS OF CONVENIENCE

*Lesson I've learned the hard way #115: Paying taxes is for suckers. I am a sucker.*

One of the most brilliant moves the cruise industry has made and profited from is the idea of registering its ships in different countries; the Men's Sexy Legs Competition being a close second. Most ships operate under "flags of convenience," which is really just an inconspicuous way of saying they can choose which country's laws and regulations they have to abide by. As I write this, the majority of ships, not surprisingly, are registered under nations whose governments don't enforce the most sophisticated of tax codes: the Bahamas, Panama, and Liberia.[8] It's essentially the cruise lines' version of offshore banking, if that comparison speaks to you. All they have to do is fly the registered country's flag on their ships, pay the those governments some nominal fees, and they can successfully avoid abiding by any U.S. laws or paying taxes. Convenient, right?

Registering a ship in, say, Liberia, has significant benefits for the U.S. shipping and cruise industries. You are subject to the laws and regulations of the flag state, meaning none of those wacky labor unions allowed, and whatever the cruise lines feel like paying you for all the work you can physically handle! In essence, that

---

[8] Febin, A.K. (2007). Evolution of Flags of Convenience. *Shipping Law Notes.*

ship is a floating piece of Liberia. Also, and this is another biggie, cruise lines only pay the taxes that the flag state requires, or, "none" in layman's terms. The cost to register a company in Liberia is roughly $4,500 US. The fees are—mockingly enough—collected by a company specially contracted to administer the Liberian register, which for decades was a little place called International Registries Incorporated. Based out of? You guessed it, America. Virginia to be specific. Tax evasion comes full circle.[9]

Let's review; these corporations hand over a few thousand dollars to a guerilla government in the third world and skirt paying the U.S. hundreds of millions of dollars in taxes annually. Ironic, as most of the revenue ships earn comes from Americans who actually do pay taxes. U.S. Taxpayers also get to foot the bill when the U.S. Coast Guard is called in the event of a hostage situation, or to investigate drugs, weapons, human trafficking, oil spills, illegal fishing, and everything else a developing nation would not necessarily consider detrimental to its existence. And so, these "Flags of Convenience" manage to single handedly fuck up Reagonomics.

But why choose *Liberia*? Is this a way for Liberians to get back at the U.S. for that whole slavery thing? Sure they offer virtually no interference from the government, no taxes and an undeniable veil of secrecy, but why not go with a place like Bhutan? I'm sure they would let you do whatever you want too and they've got a really

---

[9] Ibid.

sharp looking dragon on their flag. Maybe they went with Liberia because its flag looks so similar to the U.S. flag and they were hoping people wouldn't notice the forty-nine missing stars.

The truth is, nobody knows why Liberia was the chosen registry, nay, *I* do not know why Liberia was the chosen registry for so many years, but I can tell you it was a major contributor to the cruise industry's profits from the 1940s until about 2002. And if it weren't for that nagging United Nations declaring Liberia a pariah state due to the Charles Taylor regime's support of guerrillas in Sierra Leone's bloody civil war, it still would be. The U.S. was willing to overlook the first two civil wars you were responsible for Charles, but three strikes seems to be a good rule of thumb for breaking ties with a genocidal maniac.

Apparently U.S. cruise ships didn't feel as if funding a crazed African warlord was good for business any longer. Though the rest of the world didn't seem to care much, as Liberia remains the flag of convenience for over 3,500 ships today, second only to Panama.[10]

If retail mogul Wal-Mart were earning at Carnival Cruise lines margins, and not held accountable to paying U.S. taxes for instance, it would have made an unheard of $65 billion in profits. An amount greater than those of the world's four most profitable companies: Citigroup, GE, Bank of America, and Exxon-Mobil—*combined.* Unfortunately here on terra

---

[10] Shaw, J. Flag of Convenience—or Flag of Necessity?

firma there are laws, and Wal-Mart's profits were reported as $8 billion—minus taxes.[11]

In researching further about flags of convenience, I had the good fortune to come across a friend's "textbooks-from-college-that-I-would-rather-keep-and-never-read-than-sell-back-to-the-bookstore-for-$5" collection. After rummaging through a lot of very specific International Law, I finally stumbled upon the "Nationality of Vessels" section. Article 91 states:

> *Every State shall fix the conditions for the grant of its nationality to ships, for the registration of ships in its territory, and for the right to fly its flag. Ships have the nationality of the State whose flag they are entitled to fly. There must be a genuine link between the State and the ship.[12]*

After reading the unnecessarily wordy Law of the Sea, I was curious to clarify what exactly constitutes a genuine link between the state and the ship? And what can a State do if it knows or suspects a ship has no genuine link with the state of registration? Then I kept reading:

> *A State has a "genuine link" entitling it to register a ship and to authorize the ship to use its flag if the ship is owned by nationals of the state, whether natural or juridical persons, and the state*

---

[11] Garin, p. 207.

[12] McCaffrey, S. *The Law of International Watercourses.* 2007.

*exercises effective control over the ship. In most cases a ship is owned by a corporation created by the state of registry. However, in determining whether a 'genuine link' with the state of registry exists, the following additional factors are to be taken into account: whether the officers and crew of the ship are nationals of the state; how often the ship stops in the ports of the state; and how extensive and effective is the control that the state exercises over the ship.* [13]

First, I would challenge you to read another forty pages of similarly phrased legislature without falling asleep and/or wanting to kill yourself. Second, I would like to point out that Royal Caribbean, a U.S. company, owns the ship. Not nationals of the Bahamas, the *Voyager's* country of registry. Of the 84 nationalities of crewmembers on the ship, I cannot recall a single Bahamian passing me in the I-95. That's not to say there weren't ever any Bahamian employees onboard, just that they are certainly not a majority. The captain and staff captain were Norwegian, the human resources manager and cruise director Canadian, and the chief of security was British. As for "how often the ship stops in the ports of the state," we managed to make it to the Bahamas once in my entire contract during the transatlantic crossing. While there were no announcements made about the rich Bahamian culture and connection to Royal Caribbean, we *were* warned

---

[13] United Nations Convention on the Law of the Sea (1982). p. 54.

not to venture past the main street or *The Atlantis* resort as crime rates were soaring. Perhaps the Bahamian government should've asked for some tax money from their little floating paradise. If the control that the state exercised over the ship were effective, they probably wouldn't find themselves wrecked with poverty. The only time I even saw a Bahamian authority was when we docked there, and he was wearing a "We Be Jammin" shirt and flip-flops. Well, huh. It would appear that there is no genuine link between most of these cruise ships and their flag states, soooo why is nothing being done about it? Oh right, because it still really doesn't matter.

> *If another state doubts the existence of a genuine link, for instance, because there is evidence that the flag state has not been exercising its duties to control and regulate the ship, it may request that the flag state "investigate the matter and, if appropriate, take any action necessary to remedy the situation."[14]*

So just to clarify, there doesn't *actually* have to be a genuine link like that misleading Article 94 told us. The flag state just has to say there is. And after setting foot outside Nassau's main street, they're in no position to turn down free money, as minimal as the registration fees may be. Perhaps they too were promised by Royal Caribbean that "the registration fee may seem small now, but just wait until all the guests from

---

[14]  Ibid.

our ships spend a day, and their money, on your island." Only to find out later the ship would dock there just twice a year.

As crazy as it sounds to register a passenger ship in its *actual* country of operation, there was a time when this was standard practice. It wasn't until 1922, when William Harriman registered the ex-*German Reliance* and *Resolute* under the flag of Panama that ship owners realized they've been paying taxes to their home countries like suckers for so long.[15] What caused Harriman to think up his brilliant idea? Was he trying to evade taxes? Avoid labor laws? Help to fund the maintenance of that cool new canal he'd heard was down there? No my friends. William flew under the Panamanian flag for all the right reasons: he wanted to allow his passengers the option of getting sauced in the middle of the Atlantic.

You see, these ships were American-owned and at the time, those poindexters in Congress had the terrible judgment to let the 18th Amendment pass. So in addition to strengthening the mafia, overburdening the penal system, and hurting ugly peoples' chances of hooking up, Prohibition was also the spark that set off this entire flags of convenience ordeal, cheating the U.S. out of hundreds of millions of tax dollars a year. Not to mention all of the other terrible things that result at sea from minimal legal obligations. And so, you see how one man's noble vision of inebriating passengers transformed into quite

---

[15] Shaw, p. 1.

possibly the greatest legitimate scam in the travel industry.

Cruise lines don't get to avoid all fees associated with running a normal business however, at least not when they're caught. Various lines have paid millions of dollars for dumping wastewater, oil, photographic chemicals, solvents, dry cleaning fluids, lubricants, and sewage in some of the world's most treasured waters. Failure to operate at a slow speed near Humpback whales resulting in death? That cost Princess Cruises approximately $200,000 in fines and $550,000 in restitution.[16] Almost all fines are on a case-by-case basis, dependent upon how much oil, or hazardous waste, or trash, or paint was actually dumped into the water, if records were falsified, if the cruise line turned themselves in, or if the incident is reported back to the ship's flag state. And although an $18 million fine may sound hefty for dumping toxic chemicals and oil-contaminated water into Alaska's waters, it hardly makes a dent in Royal Caribbean's approximate $6 *billion* annual revenue.[17] Two engineers who had falsified records fled criminal charges because hey, that's the beauty of operating in international waters. As part of the plea agreement, the line agreed not to discharge wastewater within three miles of Alaska's coastline. If you happen to fish 3.1 miles off the coast of Alaska, please take note.

---

[16] Princess Lines fined in whale's death (2007). 29 Jan. 2007.

[17] Martinson, J. (1999). Cruise line fined $18m for dumping waste at sea.

After reading about some of the horrors of the cruise ship industry, you know you should hate them, but the enjoyment and convenience of the product they promote make it all too easy to turn a blind eye to some of their atrocities. Much like pretending you're unaware of the Nike sweatshops in Southeast Asia...or eating meat. And truth be told, I hate when vegetarians lecture people on the cruelty of consuming animal products, and I am not discouraging anybody from taking a cruise. They're a blast. Just hope you don't find yourself needing medical assistance on one of them.

# CHAPTER VIII: ROLLING THE DICE WITH THE HEALTH CENTER

***Lesson I've learned the hard way #157: Don't go to the health center.***

I feel obliged to give the medical center its own chapter in this book for the simple reason that it was too ridiculous not to. I cannot say enough about how terrible this place was to deal with, but for entertainment's sake, I'll try.

The medical center for crew and guests has two separate waiting rooms; they wouldn't want crewmembers later hooking up with guests that they had chatted up while waiting for a diagnosis, of course. On the other hand, the crew waiting room had a free vending machine-like dispenser complete with condoms, seasickness pills, and ibuprofen for that hangover that just won't go away. In short, everything you need for a good night and all for free! If you could get to the medical center fast enough, that was. The seasickness pills were as hot a commodity during stormy weather as the condoms were on crew party nights.

Upon entering the actual medical center, there are nurses from all over the world—about three of them— to "greet" you. I use the term "greet" loosely because it tends to have positive connotations associated with it. Perhaps "interrogate," "question your motives," and "express annoyance by your presence" may be a more appropriate description in my experience.

The nurses and doctors all hail from the greatest health care producing nations in the world: Ukraine, Philippines, Slovakia, and various other countries where you can make more money working on a cruise ship than as a doctor in your homeland.  In fact, over 95% of cruise ship doctors are not educated, trained, or licensed in the U.S.[18] Absent are the medical degrees, freethinking, common sense, or manners that you might expect to find in a real hospital (some of them at least). Present however, are free flu shots, whether or not you requested one.

When my Dutch roommate Anne had a mild case of diarrhea, they told her to bend over and injected a shot into her butt without telling her what it was, asking for her consent, or making sure she didn't have any medication allergies. We still don't know for sure if it was a flu shot. That was just deductive reasoning, as they didn't seem very familiar with many other vaccines. It is moves like this that make me question just what the requirements to be a ship nurse or doctor are on Royal Caribbean, or any other ship for that matter. Does anybody regulate ship medical centers?

A little research would show that the American College of Emergency Physicians (ACEP) has set forth "guidelines and qualifications" for emergency physicians, such as those found on cruise ships, but the cruise ship is under no obligation to follow these. In fact, as

---

[18] Walker, J. (2011). Fox News Focuses on Dangerous Cruise Ship Medical Care.

mentioned earlier, most ships operate under "flags of convenience," which means they can choose which country's laws and regulations they have to abide by.

Of course this means ship's medical facilities and staff are "regulated" by the third world country of which they are registered to, the majority of which were the Bahamas, Panama and Liberia. Assuming one of these countries is say, in a civil war for decades, they probably don't spend much time making sure a cruise ship's syringes are sterile, nothing that a small bribe couldn't rectify regardless, but that's just a hypothesis. Now I hate to assume the worst, despite my seemingly skeptical views on the medical center, but nothing about it led me to believe these people were certified to practice medicine in countries whose population didn't rely on witch doctors.

A survey conducted in 1999 as part of a *New York Times* investigation found that fewer than 60 percent of the doctors aboard Carnival Cruise Lines ships had the credentials necessary to work in a U.S. hospital.[19] In fact, it wasn't until 1998, under pressure from the American Medical Association, that the International Council of Cruise Lines (ICCL) adopted a set of guidelines with "input" from the American College of Emergency Physicians. Unfortunately for posterity's sake, these policies were voluntary, neither enforced nor inspected by the ICCL.[20] One ill-fated 47-year-old woman had a heart attack

---

[19] Garin, p. 265-266.
[20] Ibid.

misdiagnosed as bronchitis subsequent to these policies being "adopted." Probably not a problem too many stateside docs have, given the simplicity of conducting an EKG, but both can manifest themselves in chest pains and shortness in breath, so it's possible that a professor in a medical school wouldn't fail a student for such a diagnosis. But then there was another case of a diabetic passenger that went into a coma and, after the ship doctor misread his diagnostic equipment, administered a near-lethal dose of glucose instead of the insulin she so desperately needed, resulting in brain damage.[21] Maybe the doctors were trying to close the knowledge gap.

Another incident in 1997 involved a doctor on the Carnival ship Ecstasy diagnosing a fourteen-year-old girl with—their specialty—the flu (no information was given as to whether or not the girl was given a pregnancy test as well, we'll assume from the anecdote about Jessie below that she was). Turns out the girl had appendicitis, which left untreated, leads to shockingly high mortality rates. The doctor was so sure it was the flu that he didn't bother checking the girl further, despite her mother asking him "point blank" if the girl's appendix could be the problem.[22] The doctor admitted that he was not sure what it was, but did confirm that it was *not* the girl's appendix, right before he apologized for their vacation being ruined. Now if those aren't top-notch bedside manners I don't know what are.

---

[21] Ibid.
[22] Ibid.

Perhaps what the doctor *should* have said in court when the family sued for medical malpractice was, "Sorry for prescribing your daughter antibiotics for a stomach virus instead of confirming your worries that she did indeed have appendicitis. Sorry that she nearly died because of my negligence. And sorry that due to the lack of immediate medical attention your daughter is now sterile and incapable of ever having children." I'm sure the doc would've said something along these terms had he made an appearance in court. While filing the suit, attorneys for the girl's family had come to find that the doctor had fled town. But don't worry; it is not all that unlikely that you will see him in the infirmary of another cruise line. In fact, it turns out that you or I, or Dr. Kevorkian, could also be your next healthcare provider on a ship! It was revealed in the lawsuit that Carnival had not followed up on any of the doctor's references when he had applied for the job. I've had *Subway* check my references for Christ's sake.

There have been several examples of the medical center's perennial shortcomings on ships, which, considering the cruise industry's seemingly innate ability to keep such blunders from ever being publicized, most likely represent only a small proportion of those that actually happen.

As mentioned earlier, I managed to avoid getting my hepatitis C test done for over a month through a combination of meeting with the H.R. manager and avoiding the medical center after we landed on American soil, which is when I was supposed to get it done. As it turns out, my health insurance only covers these tests if done during my annual check up, which my ever-so-thorough doctor neglected to do. By this time however, I had developed a seriously concerning cough. You know, the type where you laugh and it quickly turns into a whooping cough-like fit that makes it sound like you've been smoking three packs a day since exiting the womb. If you have any friends with emphysema you know what I'm talking about. But I was in that small third percentile of crewmembers that did not smoke, which led me to believe that this cough was brought on by those carcinogenic black flakes of God-knows-what that would occasionally blow in our faces from the ship's smokestacks as we belayed at the rock wall. Typically I would wait out a cough, and the fact that I had to avoid the medical center due to that hep C debacle solidified that strategy for nearly six weeks, at which point I realized that this cough was not going away. So finally I caved and got my hepatitis C test done in Cozumel for $70 (if you're reading this, Dr. Powers, I still plan on sending you that bill), and returned to the medical center the next day to get checked out.

I should mention that, like many other amenities available to the crewmembers, there is a small window of opportunity to take advantage of such services. Make no mistake, the medical center is certainly no exception to this and is open from 8 a.m.-9 a.m. and 4 p.m.-5 p.m. for crewmembers. Should you fall ill at any of the other 22 hours of the day, I'm not really sure what would happen. I do know however, that you need to get a slip from your supervisor before seeing any kind of a doctor, because why cut out the middle man when your health is failing?

As you may have guessed, I was scheduled to work during both of the medical center's hours of operation; even skipping lunch wasn't an option. And so I began to jump through Royal Caribbean's hoops and convinced my supervisor to let me out of work fifteen minutes early and sign my doctor's slip so I could consult somebody who would be able to help me more than WebMD. As it turns out, that kind of help is not available on the ship.

I entered the medical center and was greeted by a nurse with a clipboard who immediately made her hatred for me evident, either because of that entire hep C incident or because I was seeking medical attention fifteen minutes before close. Although, that would've only been 45 minutes into her shift, so we'll assume it was the former. After actually reading the disclaimer on the clipboard, which I could tell she was not used to people doing and was quite perturbed by, I handed it back to her.

"You need to sign here," she said and placed the clipboard down in front of me less than gently. I re-read the part that I needed to sign; it read something along the lines of "the doctor has demonstrated/explained how and when to take any medications you have been given."

After thinking back on the ten seconds I had been in the medical center, it had occurred to me that this information had never been communicated to me.

"But I haven't even seen a doctor yet," I told her confused.

"Just sign it!" she snapped at me as if she was about to go into labor any minute and didn't have time to explain to me why I should sign her sheet of lies. It didn't look like I was going make it past the waiting room if I didn't succumb to her wishes, so I signed the waiver.

Upon entering the doctor's office, I was really just hoping he could give me some medicine that would allow me to inhale without hacking up a lung in the future, but instead he handed me an unmarked bag of unmarked pills along with a generic version of Nyquil and decided to confine me.

Confinement, for those of you not familiar with the process on the ship, is exactly what it sounds like. You are confined for a minimum amount of time and not allowed to leave your room until the doctor has OK'd you. The minimum confinement time varies depending on your illness. For instance, if you go to the doc complaining of diarrhea, you shouldn't have. Gastrointestinal infections go for a minimum seven days of confinement. This may sound like a nice little break after you've been working everyday for five months, but I would liken it more to spending a week in jail.

The first day you can catch up on movies on the crew channel, read a book, write postcards if you have them, clean your room, take a shower and catch up on much needed sleep. After you realize you've seen every movie twice and begin to forget what the sun looks like, you start to show effects similar to those in the Stanford Prison experiment. And being restricted to a room the size of a shoebox with very limited ventilation and stale, germ-infested air literally gives you cabin fever. Which is unfortunate for your roommate, who also has to breathe that air and see a doctor if you are confined.

Of course, if they determine you are extra contagious, they will put you in your own special room where you are not allowed to have any kind of human interaction. With the exception of the room service waiter, donning a SARS mask, you are completely by yourself. So being sick on a ship is awfully similar to one of the worst punishments one can receive in prison, or at least it would be if they enforced it. I've heard it's grounds for termination if you are caught leaving a confined room or visiting somebody who is supposed to be in isolation, but nobody informed me of this before breaking both of those rules.

I was shocked that I was confined at all, seeing as how I had had this cough for nearly six weeks and any damage that was going to be done by it had already been done. I was especially mad that I had been confined because I had just finished work for the day and was planning on celebrating Australia Day that night. The only benefit to being confined, other than missing work, was room service. Evidently there is a special "confined menu" for those of us who don't really deserve room service but are receiving it as a necessity to life. Apparently RCI doesn't think that pizza has the magical healing effects that I think it does. They also don't treat their sick with any sort of priority.

When the doctor came the next morning at 8 a.m. I was dressed and ready to go to work when he dealt me the blow. It went a little something like this, "Do you still have your cough?"

"Yes."

"Ok I'm going to confine you for the day, come to see me tomorrow at 8 a.m."

"Seriously?"

Door slam.

Once I picked my jaw up off the ground I turned toward my spotless room and pondered what I could possibly fill up the next 24 hours with. I had already finished two books and played my guitar until my fingers bled. Turns out, room service would take a significant portion of my free time. I hadn't realized when I ordered dinner the night before, because most guests go to the dining room and don't order in. But when it comes to delivering room service, sick crewmembers who are not physically allowed to get their own meals are the lowest point on the hospitality totem pole. I ordered a bagel and cream cheese at 9 a.m. and it didn't come until 11:15 a.m. There are apparently quite a few guests who can't find it in their strength to get out of bed and walk the 50 feet to breakfast. And honestly I can't say I would be any different on vacation, especially when breakfast closes before noon. But that doesn't alleviate any bitterness I had about waiting two hours for a bagel.

I used all the resources I had available to entertain me for the rest of the day, which included sculpting *The David* out of play-doh, blowing the biggest bubble of gum I have ever blown in my life, and attempting to fashion a slinky out of my roommate's metal clothes hangers, among other things. I called it a night at about 7:00 p.m. with the hope that a day and a half of confinement in a stale cabin and some unmarked pills had magically cured my six week cough and the doctor would allow me to see the light of day tomorrow. It did not of course, but luckily the doctor did not care. I hadn't coughed loudly in his presence and so he decided the treatment had worked. I had talked them into giving me the nebulizer once more for my personal enjoyment, and as I took a shortcut to the room I couldn't help but notice a "blue boy" (the ship's term for the deck hands, all of whom are from third world or developing nations and brought there to work as many thankless hours as their bodies would allow in sharp blue jumpsuits) sitting on the examining table.

I went to "greet and smile" as RCI so lovingly encourages, at which point I noticed he was grasping his hand, which was significantly lighter now that it was missing a thumb. This probably wouldn't have been nearly as noticeable if it hadn't been gushing blood. Choking back my gag reflex, I gave a half-hearted smile; the kind that says I'd rather be tending to a "code brown" in the youth center's Adventure Ocean than right here, right now. If that wasn't subtle enough, I also completely turned around and decided that the long way would do just fine; after all, there was a volcano of blood pouring out of this man's hand and I know first hand how easy it is to get on this ship with hepatitis C. Okay, that's not exactly what was going through my mind at the time, but I wanted to leave the man a little privacy. It's not everyday you lose your Goddamn fingers.

I also got the eerie impression that I wasn't meant to see that, so when I walked past the doctors and nurses on my way to the exit, I tried my best to deemphasize the fact that I had just witnessed an unlucky soul literally chopped down in his prime. I should note that he was a good sport about the whole situation and was at the crew bar later that night, complete with bandages on his severed thumb.

I pretty much steered clear of the medical center after that, with the exception of needing an occasional tube of hydrocortisone cream from that rash brought on by my nametag. Aside from not wanting to run into anymore limbless patients, their track record was not exactly ideal.

Eating lunch one day at the mess hall, my friend Jessie, a youth staff manager, sat at my table looking less than exceptional. She had the same face as one of my friends right after we drove as fast as we could around a rotary in Cape Cod a record breaking seventeen times. Well, the look she had right before emptying the contents of her stomach on the side of the Mass Pike at least.

I asked Jessie if she was feeling seasick and she replied that she's been working on ships for four years and has never succumbed to that nauseating feeling that only Mother Nature and an unstable ship can produce. "So what do you think is wrong? Did you go to the medical center?"

Her reply was five seconds of silence combined with a look asking me not to humor her. That was followed by her all too familiar, disappointing encounter with the medical center. She had been feeling nauseous for about three weeks now (it's amazing how slow sicknesses are to heal on the ship), and this was the third time she had been to the medical center. The first time they gave her seasickness pills and a pregnancy test, despite her protests that there was absolutely no chance she was pregnant. They sent her on her way with what sounds like the same unmarked bag of pills I received for my whooping cough; the panacea of all ship diseases.

Jessie's second visit to the medical center was predictably redundant. They asked her again if she was seasick.

"No, I've worked on ships for four years and have yet to get seasick."

"Sometimes bodies change."

"Yes, I understand that, but I feel like this on land too," Jessie replied.

"Hmm…I think you might be pregnant, we'll need to test for that."

And so they confirmed for a second time that Jessie was not indeed pregnant. But they did not actually figure out what was wrong with her. In fact, I'm not sure if they considered anything other than seasickness or pregnancy. But hey, they were busy sewing fingers back on to very underpaid workers, get off their backs.

Attempt number three of Jessie's relentless quest for a proper medical evaluation over the course of three weeks was about as successful as

Roseanne Barr's infamous performance of the National Anthem at a 1990 Padres game. Though they did see fit to test if she was pregnant again (guess what?—she wasn't), they never did actually figure out what was wrong with poor Jessie. A week or two after she told me this story, Jessie would leave the ship the way she boarded it—the way too many people do—without notice and in a state of disarray.

Perhaps what was more confusing about why the medical center would test three times for pregnancy despite there being no chance of it, was the case of "Vera Feraro and the mysterious skin disease." The origin of the skin disease was determined to be a beach in Costa Maya, Mexico. Vera had been there with friends, all of who swam in the same ocean, laid in the same sand, ate at the same restaurant, the list goes on. When Vera came back to the ship however, after a few hours she noticed an unsightly rash on her hands and arms. When the irritation didn't go away after a few days, she decided to test her luck at the health center. I would liken a correct diagnosis at the health center to a scratch ticket: more likely than winning the lottery, but still not the kind of odds you would like to see, especially when dealing with your health. Alas, Vera did not win her scratch ticket. What was more appalling was that they judged it to be chicken pox, which, as anybody who has looked up anything about chicken pox in the second grade when their mother led a relentless quest to get her child infected with the disease could tell you, it certainly was not.[23]

As you may know, chicken pox generally tends to manifest itself in blisters and rashes that itch like hell. It's also usually associated with a fever, fatigue, abdominal pain, sore throat, and nausea—none of which Vera suffered from. Either the detectives at the medical center get pleasure from confining people, or the breadth of their medical knowledge comes from a "most common health problems on a cruise ship" pamphlet courtesy of the Seven Seas Group.

Vera was confined, nay, isolated in her own deserted room on floor 0 for about five or six days. It took us two days to learn this information, and another day to discover which room she was banished to. I went to visit her on day 4, which I would come to learn, is strictly forbidden. This protocol was one of the few things that actually made sense about the medical center. After all, if they thought you were contagious with something as serious as chicken pox, I can understand why they would not want other employees breathing the same disease-riddled air as you. Fortunately for me, I've got the sort of confidence in my immune system where I don't see it necessary to follow these completely sensible rules. That, and the rationale that I had several interactions with her before she was confined, and if I was going to catch whatever the hell it was that she had, I

---

[23] When I finally did catch chicken pox after one particularly germ-laden play date with five of the sickest children my mother could find, she claimed the disease has worse affects on adults and was "doing it for my own good." That would provide little solace when I saw the chicken pox vaccine advertised a few years later.

would've caught it by now. Besides, I wasn't going to let a little bout of leprosy stop me from winning back my UNO title.

Had I known the penalty (immediate dismissal) for the rule I wasn't aware I was about to break, I probably would have been a little more covert. I swear this ship's designer was chosen from some architecture competition at the Academy for the Blind whose blueprints existed solely to make everybody else's life difficult. I must've ascended and descended three different sets of staircases in my effort to find her room, looking completely confused all the while, and asking for directions on more than one occasion. Apparently the suggestion to build a floor that you can walk to from end to end without encountering walls or staircases was deemed "too convenient." Once the sensation that I was in a real life game of Zelda had passed, I entered the isolation room to find Vera reading what looked like her fifteenth magazine. She had also completed several books, watched every movie on the crew channel and written an uncanny amount of postcards. I didn't know it was possible to get that many postcards past security for fear that you were creating some sort of postcard bomb.

Aside from the cabin fever, Vera seemed fine. No fever, no nausea, no stomach pains, but unfortunately no improvement in that vicious skin disease that seemed to be spreading like a bad case of herpes. At this point, I wasn't sure if she was being isolated because she was sick or because it would scare the children. I kid, it wasn't *that* bad, but bad enough to dissuade any of us from returning to that beach ever again. I did notice the trademark bag of unmarked pills that's passed out by the medical center like candy at a parade. She was granted ship leave in Cozumel to see somebody more familiar with medicine than RCI's finest. The local middle school biology class was very helpful.

The doctors at Cozumel Health were familiar with the rash, and although they weren't sure where it originated or what caused it, they had a cure. I found this dynamic fascinating, alchemy at its finest. Sure there could've been a few deaths when testing it out, and who knows the long term effects, but let's be honest, who really cares? It'll make that unsightly rash vanish in time for high tide next week. And this is what I love about Mexicans. They don't worry about the long-term health effects of adding Sweet N' Low to your coffee or replacing your water intake with Corona at least twice a day. They subscribe to the carpe diem mantra that our Latin friends so fervently adopted years ago. And I will say this much, it makes for a far more enjoyable life than constantly worrying about if talking on your cell phone is setting you up for life as a vegetable when that tumor develops and metastasizes.[24]

---

[24] The police in Mexico seem to embrace this maxim as well, and what a breathe of fresh air that was. Not once did I ever fear being pulled over on a rented scooter for going above the speed limit, and this wasn't just because our scooters barely went the speed limit (actually we don't really know how fast they went, the speedometers were broken), but because they're a little more lax than policemen from the United States. I've had friends pulled

My qualms with Royal Caribbean's medical staff could go on and on, but for time and litigation purposes I will simply end with the quote, "It is a mathematical fact that fifty percent of all doctors graduate in the bottom half of their

---

over for having too much tint in her window, not having his seat belt on, talking on the phone while driving, not having a front license plate (ticketed twice in a 24 hour period), expired plates, taillights out, not signaling, not stopping for a complete three seconds at a stop sign, passing a school bus that was about to stop, driving too fast, driving too slow, not driving with an adult in the car, driving with too many adults in the car, etc. And this is only a percentage of the traffic violations you can rack up in the land of the free. I actually know somebody who was ticketed for jaywalking in Ohio. Now up until then I honestly didn't believe that jaywalking was a ticket-able offense. In fact, up until I was twelve I probably thought it was a dance of some sort. What kind of law would prohibit people from crossing a street? If it's in place to protect the people then why are you ticketing them? If it's in place to protect the drivers, I think they'll be alright in their two-ton block of metal on wheels. So either some guy named Jay really wanted the stupidest law of all time named after him and really pushed for it, or it's simply a way of funding a police department's slow-pitch softball team.

I'm not in any way promoting the Mexican police force as a model to be followed, because that is far from the truth. I'm just saying it's nice to be able to take the cap off of a beer on a public sidewalk without worrying about being cuffed and thrown into a squad car. This laissez-faire approach to all matters of life is why I love you, Mexico. With that said, I hope I never actually need to rely on the Mexican police to help me. Not like their creative doctors, whose skin concoction managed to eradicate Vera's rash in no time.

class"—many of whom now call cruise ships home.

# CHAPTER IX: TRAGEDIES AT SEA

*Lesson I've learned the hard way #165: Morgues are as much of a necessity on cruise ships as 24-hour pizza buffets.*

As far as industries go, cruise ships remain relatively elusive in terms of incriminating information. Much like Ronald Reagan, nothing negative ever seems to stick to them, no matter how many scandals occur. Reading about fires, muggings, sexual assaults, missing persons, murders, pirate attacks, and misdiagnoses of serious illnesses by ship doctors will leave you less concerned with the lighter issues that may befall cruise ships, like cockroaches and bed bugs. Such are the claims of one of the only websites dedicated to providing information about the "other side" of cruising, a helpful and cleverly named website: www.cruisebruise.com.

To further the rhyme scheme, the "Cruise Bruise News" consists of anything anybody could ever want to know about horrific tales while cruising. Husbands throwing their wives overboard, a Captain using his master key to break into a 13-year-old passenger's room and sexually assault her, a ship nurse being locked up for disagreeing with a doctor's treatment; this is the website the cruise industries don't want you to see. And the truth is, most of you won't. I don't have the statistics, but I think it's safe to say "Fatally beaten wives on cruise ships" is not one of the top searches on Google. And the truth is, unless you have a vested interest in it, say…if you were writing a book on it, it is not exactly a subject that comes up during water cooler talk.

While there is enough information on Cruise Bruise to fill an entire shelf of books, one story of a "missing" person struck a more personal chord with me, as I seemed to have heard it before.

January 2, 2010

## Passenger Overboard On New Year's Eve Is Crew Member's Wife

Neha Chhikara, 23, was aboard Monarch of the Seas in the Caribbean on New Year's Eve, when she went overboard from the port side 11th deck around 0411 hours on Thursday, December 31, 2009.

Chhikara was reported missing by her husband, a crewmember aboard the cruise ship, shortly after midnight. Mrs. Chhikara was last seen alive around 0345 hours.

She was the last overboard person for 2009, in what had been an unusually busy year for cruise industry search and rescue operations.

Royal Caribbean Cruise Lines' Monarch of The Seas had embarked from Port Canaveral, in Cape Canaveral, Florida on Monday, December 28, 2009 for a five-day voyage. The ship was en route to Little Stirrup Cay from Nassau, Bahamas.[25]

---

[25] Walker, J. (2010). Update on Death of Royal Caribbean Crew Member Neha Chhikara.

First, I would like to point out how awed I am that the last overboard person of 2009 came in with a whole 20 hours to spare in the year. Second, this report stuck out to me because I remember hearing about it via the crew hotline (word of mouth, there is not actually a phone number we can call to get this information) when I was on the *Voyager*. Word had spread like wildfire (the only way word spreads through a ship) that an Indian woman had jumped overboard after being mentally and physically beaten by her husband, a Royal Caribbean employee. Turns out that rumor was eerily accurate, and Neha had reportedly sent her brother an email from the ship stating, "Ankit has been beating me every day on the ship. I have lost the strength to live."[26] Neha's husband, RCI employee Ankit Dalal, reported his wife missing eight hours after she had jumped to her death, the investigation started nearly 12 hours after the incident. You could have watched Dexter Morgan kill ten people in that kind of time!

The Dalal family was allegedly harassing Neha for not bringing enough dowry to the marriage; ironic, as the historical purpose of paying a dowry is to help a husband feed and protect his family and to give the wife and children support if he were to die. Either Ankit had a really roundabout way of "protecting" his family, or he was a less glamorous wife beater employed on RCI's *Monarch of the Seas*, a

---

[26] See reference 21...for pretty much everything regarding this story.

residence whose law jurisdiction is as fuzzy as Royal Caribbean's background checks.

Neha's family wanted the Dalal's arrested for dowry harassment, but Indian authorities could not take action due to the incident occurring out of the country. But don't worry; Indian justice would be carried out. The Deputy Commissioner of Police later said that the police would book Ankit for dowry death when Neha's death is confirmed. Perfect. Nothing like waiting for your daughter's corpse to turn up on a shore so the man who is responsible for her death can serve his time for it. And we all know the chances of a human body turning up after years in the ocean are about as good as India getting rid of a dowry system anytime soon.

Neither investigating authorities (the FBI and Bahamas Maritime Authority) have provided any information to the family nor the Indian police. The cruise line is not cooperating with the family and does not even know where the RCI crewmember is as of January 6, 2010, less than a week after the incident. The Indian police are waiting to hear back from either authority before continuing their investigation, and as the *Monarch of the Seas* is sailing under the flags of the Bahamas, their reports are likely to be skewed in favor of the organization that pays them. And just like that, the cruise ship industry remains untouched by yet another murky event that occurred on a ship in their fleet. What's more, if you are not in the small percentage of people who will read this book, or who were on the ship at the time Neha jumped, you will most likely never know about "incidents" like this that are far too common in the industry with no accountability.

While rapes, murders, and drug smugglers may slip under the radar, there was at least one story that made international headlines for its astounding incompetence. Depending on how long it takes me to actually find a publisher for this book, you may remember what critics and passengers likened to a second *Titanic* catastrophe. At about 10:30 p.m. CET on January 13, 2012, just off the coast of Tuscany, Italy, the Carnival-owned *Costa Concordia* managed to crash into—of all things—the ground. That's right, it wasn't a massive hurricane, an iceberg, or a German U-boat that took this ship down, the Captain literally drove it into the ground. The sharp reef in the Mediterranean managed to slash a 50-meter hole in the hull of the ship, causing it to take on water rapidly enough for the Captain himself to abandon it as soon as possible. Fortunately, the ship wasn't in the middle of the frigid North Atlantic hundreds of miles from any kind of help, and the people who jumped overboard (see, the fall didn't kill them) were able to swim to shore.

When I first read about this disaster, I was confused as to why it was getting so much press. There have been dozens of shipwrecks in the past thirty years, many of which suffered higher casualty rates, and most of which I had never heard of before researching the issue for this book. Why had I never heard of "The Great *Al Salam Boccaccio 98* Tragedy of 2006" in which the Egyptian ferry sank in the Red Sea and took with it the lives of nearly 1000 Egyptians on their way home from work in Saudi Arabia?[27] Can you imagine the world hearing nothing about 1000 commuters perishing as they took the Ferry from Manhattan to Staten Island?

Or why has nobody I've asked ever heard of the *MS Estonia,* sinking in 1994 and killing 852 mostly Scandinavian passengers?[28] Not to trivialize the loss of two-dozen lives, but more people have died at a soccer game in England than the number who died from *Concordia's* sinking. So why is it that so much coverage was given to the *Concordia*? After hearing tales of some horrific stories (people passing their babies off to safety when they didn't think they would make it, crawling through hallways with nothing but the light of the life vest to guide them, plates smashing against the ground as the ship capsized etc.), maybe it was just better TV. Or maybe it was the fact that it could have been any number of us on that ship.

At any given moment, there are over 200,000 people cruising the high seas. The *Concordia,* you see, is strikingly similar to the *Voyager.* At the time of her construction she was the largest Italian cruise ship ever built. She has a capacity of 3,700 passengers and 1,100 crew, is roughly the same length, and has remarkably similar amenities. Perhaps the most startling aspect about this shipwreck (aside from the fact

---

[27] McCarthy, R. (2006). 1,000 feared dead as ferry sinks in Red Sea.

[28] Langewiesche, W. (2004). A Sea Story.

that shipwrecks like this are still happening in 2012), is that despite all of the maritime laws requiring crew and passenger drills, there was still utter chaos and absolutely no leadership. Hell, even the captain abandoned the ship before the passengers. That's never good.

Aside from hitting a giant reef a few hours after departure, quite possibly the biggest problem was that nobody knew what to do. International law requires that a muster drill be held within 24 hours of leaving the first port. Not quite the best thought out plan, given the possibility that an emergency could happen, say, *within* the first 24 hours. The *Concordia* departed from Civitavecchia, Italy at approximately 7:00 p.m. on January 13, 2012. The ship's muster drill was not scheduled until 5:00 p.m. on January 14, 2012, but the crash occurred a mere 3.5 hours post departure. Hence, shear chaos and hysteria on a sinking ship.

Now I've never really been sure how much passengers take away from those muster drills, week after week I would see people talking to each other, sleeping on chairs they claimed they needed for "physical reasons," and doing anything else they could to avoid paying attention to the emergency instructions. I regarded them as similar to the safety drills flight attendants give before takeoff, the only people who pay attention are those who have never flown before or were convinced that their karmic debt was about to be repaid. Unlike an airplane crash however, ships have a much higher survival rate, given the fact that you're not plummeting out of the sky and all, so a safety drill on the high seas somehow doesn't seem as futile.

In every muster drill that I've been a part of people have acted cordially, holding doors for others, picking up a pen for someone who has dropped it, and laughing with new pals about to set out on a weeklong adventure. It's amazing how much can change when their actual lives actually seem threatened. Often in emergencies, people assume that it is just a drill and pay it no mind. Such is what happened with the Boland Hall fire at Seton Hall in which three students perished in a fire they assumed was a false alarm. But that seemed to be the opposite of what went down on the *Costa Concordia.* People reacted with panic almost from the start. One particularly selfish magician—who was in the middle of his act at the time—pulled a less than impressive vanishing act in which he failed to reappear, leaving his female assistant in a trick box,[29] possibly the safest place to be on stage when everything came crashing down I suppose. He was then seen shimmying down a ladder to safety. Who says chivalry is dead? International waters don't count— everybody knows that.

Elsewhere on the *Concordia*, people fought to get into lifeboats, the elderly and children were shoved out of the way lending credence to Darwin's "survival of the fittest" theory, and the Captain even encouraged a pregnant woman to stay aboard while he

---

[29] Sawer, P. Duffin, C. Malnick, E. & Mendick, R. (2012). Costa Concordia: The inside story of the night of Friday, January, 13.

abandoned his own handiwork before guests. All in all, it was a dark day for humanity.

If there is any silver lining in the situation—and no, I'm not talking about cheaper cruises on *Costa*—it's that there will be, wait for it, accountability! Captain Francesco Schettino, or the "Chicken of the Sea" as Italian newspapers have nicknamed him, is accused of multiple counts of manslaughter, causing a shipwreck, and abandoning the ship before all guests have been evacuated. The transcripts between Schettino and the Italian coast guard were made public shortly after the disaster and there has never been a point in my life where I had wished I spoke Italian more. Okay, that one time I thought I was ordering chicken in Italian and wound up with what looked like an organ scavenged from the black market may have topped it, but this was a close second. Sure they translated the script to English for the news, but similar to the way the film *Knocked Up* became *One Night, Big Belly* in Chinese, some things are just lost in translation.

—De Falco (Coast Guard Commander): "This is De Falco speaking from Livorno. Am I speaking with the commander?"

—Schettino: "Yes. Good evening, Commander De Falco."

—De Falco: "Please tell me your name."

—Schettino: "I'm Commander Schettino, commander"

—De Falco: "Schettino? Listen Schettino. There are people trapped onboard. Now you go with your boat under the prow on the starboard side. There is a pilot ladder. You will climb that ladder and go on board. You go on board and then you will tell me how many people there are. Is that clear? I'm recording this conversation, Commander Schettino..."

—Schettino: "Commander, let me tell you one thing..."

—De Falco: "Speak up! Put your hand in front of the microphone and speak more loudly, is that clear?"

—Schettino: "In this moment, the boat is tipping..."

—De Falco: "I understand that, listen, there are people that are coming down the pilot ladder of the prow. You go up that pilot ladder, get on that ship and tell me how many people are still on board. And what they need. Is that clear? You need to tell me if there are children, women or people in need of assistance. And tell me the exact number of each of these categories. Is that clear? Listen Schettino, you saved yourself from the sea, but I am going to...really do something bad to you...I am going to make you pay for this. Go onboard, (expletive)!"

—Schettino: "Commander, please..."

—De Falco: "No, please. You get up and go onboard now. They are telling me that onboard there are still..."

—Schettino: "I am here with the rescue boats, I am here, I am not going anywhere, I am here..."

—De Falco: "What are you doing, commander?"

—Schettino: "I am here to coordinate the rescue..."

—De Falco: "What are you coordinating there? Go on board! Coordinate the rescue from aboard the ship. Are you refusing?"

—Schettino: "No, I am not refusing."

—De Falco: "Are you refusing to go aboard commander? Can you tell me the reason why you are not going?"

—Schettino: "I am not going because the other lifeboat is stopped."

—De Falco: "You go aboard. It is an order. Don't make any more excuses. You have declared 'abandon ship.' Now I am in charge. You go on board! Is that clear? Do you hear me? Go, and call me when you are aboard. My air rescue crew is there."

—Schettino: "Where are your rescuers?"

—De Falco: "My air rescue is on the prow. Go. There are already bodies, Schettino"

—Schettino: "How many bodies are there?"

—De Falco: "I don't know. I have heard of one. You are the one who has to tell me how many there are. Christ."

—Schettino: "But do you realize it is dark and here we can't see anything..."

—De Falco: "And so what? You want to go home, Schettino? It is dark and you want to go home? Get on that prow of the boat using the pilot ladder and tell me what can be done, how many people there are and what their needs are. Now!"

—Schettino: "...I am with my second in command."

—De Falco: "So both of you go up then ... You and your second go on board now. Is that clear?"

—Schettino: "Commander, I want to go on board, but it is simply that the other boat here ... there are other rescuers. It has stopped and is waiting..."

—De Falco: "It has been an hour that you have been telling me the same thing. Now, go on board. Go on board! And then tell me immediately how many people there are there."

—Schettino: "OK, commander."

—De Falco: "Go, immediately!"[30]

I don't know whether to laugh or cry after reading this transcript. I can only imagine what was said before translation:

—Schettino: I would love to go back on the ship Commander De Falco, but you see, it's dark out here. And my second in command is with me sooooo I think we're just gonna chill here until it's not so dark. Man it's dark. Also, the boat is sort of tipping over...looks like a preeeetty sticky situation...it's probably best if we didn't add any weight to it, don't you think commander?

—De Falco: GET ON THE @#$%^&# BOAT YOU @#$%^&@, #$@%*!!!

—Schettino: Ahhhh.....yeah um, about that. Did I not mention already that it's dark?

—De Falco: #@$%@^%#^$@%#()*#$)@!!!

—Schettino: And sir, commander sir, it looks like one of the lifeboats has stopped, soooo yeah. But I can't *really* tell if it stopped because it's so dark.

—De Falco: Schettino, what the $#%^ are you telling me about the lifeboat stopping for? Is that supposed to be an excuse not to go back onboard?

---

[30] Costa Concordia transcript: Coastguard orders captain to return to stricken ship. (2012).

Why the $#%^ are you still here!? You know this conversation is being taped right? Audible evidence of you refusing to go back on your $#%^@&* ship, so there is no possible way to claim that you were the last to leave. You will look like such a $%@#$^ douche. Do you understand?!

—Schettino: Okay commander.

—De Falco: Go, immediately!

After Schettino was ordered sixteen, count 'em *sixteen* times to get back on the ship, he still refused to return, choosing instead to "coordinate the rescue" from the comfort and safety of dry land. After claiming several times that he was the last to leave the ship, he then remembered that maybe instead of *that* scenario, he had actually—and I'm not making this up—slipped, tumbled overboard and fell into a lifeboat. Well there you have it, this has just been one *huge* misunderstanding. The Captain was trying to save people when he slipped and fell into a boat, and was probably hindered from getting back out because it was so dark, mystery solved. All he's guilty of is poor balance. Since when is *that* a crime Italy?

Seriously? I know Italians are known more for their pizza and shoddily constructed towers than their fast thinking but *this* is the plan that his lawyer came up with? Couldn't he have been beamed to land by evil aliens who were out to get him for a late payment on a bet? Or didn't he really jump into the water to save one of the *Jersey Shore* kids from drowning, breaking his leg upon impact with the water and rendering him physically incapable of returning to the ship? He may have gotten more creativity points with those at least. In any event, De Falco became Italy's unlikely hero for his disparaging remarks to Captain Schettino and "Vada a bordo, cazzo!" (loosely translated as Get back on the fucking ship!) has helped ease Italy's economic crisis by appearing on banners, aprons, tee shirts and throw pillows for sale. I'll be sure to order the matching "Go fuck yourself" blankets for my grandma.

As I mentioned earlier, the *Concordia* sinking garnered quite the swarm of media attention, and one of those outlets took form in a *20/20* special titled *Cruise Ship Confidential.* The name was taken from a book written in 2008 by Brian David Bruns, a white American who had worked on a cruise ship. Huh. It details his contract on the *Carnival Conquest* (the world's largest ship at the time), describing the harsh working conditions, managerial abuses of power, and hazards of the industry. Now I know what you're thinking, "Man I wish somebody would write a slightly more modern version of the exact same book with a more colorful cover and pop culture references because we all know how much better sequels have been historically." And so alas, this book is my gift to you. Who cares if he was interviewed on national television for the piece on the *Concordia* as the sole representative of crewmembers everywhere? Not me. And so what if his book may be developed into a feature length film that will most likely exempt him from working hard ever again? All I have to do is choose a lucky combination of 6 numbers for that. Simple. Now I know what that guy who truly invented the light bulb but didn't patent it until *after* Thomas Edison felt like. What was his name again?

Back to the *20/20* special and Brian Bruns telling my story in less entertaining terms. There was actually a clip where Michael Crye, whose LinkedIn profile describes him as the Executive Vice President of Cruise Line International Association, claims that out of 100 million passengers in the past seven years, there have only been sixteen maritime related deaths (excluding 2012 of course[31]). In four months, there were multiple deaths on my ship alone. Sorry M.C., I'm gonna have to call bullshit on that.

According to the morbidly labeled "cruiseshipdeaths.com," there were 38 deaths in 2007 alone. In 2008, there were 29; 36 in 2009; 44 in 2010; and 57 in 2011. Combined with 2006 and 2005, that brings the total death toll to 262 in the past seven years.[32] Maybe by "maritime related" deaths he meant King Triton literally ripped them into the water—I didn't read all of the obituaries so that may be true. But when most people heard him quote that number, they are undoubtedly thinking people who died on a cruise ship. While

---

[31] Cuomo, C. (Reporter). (2012, January 20). Cruise Ship Confidential [Television series episode]. In *20/20*. ABC.
[32] http://www.cruiseshipdeaths.com/Deaths_By_Date

this number doesn't include the persons missing at sea, it does include the sickly group of seniors who go on a cruise ship specifically to die—not cool by the way—so we'll say they balance out. A good amount of those deaths were man overboards. How one falls off a massive cruise liner without being pushed is a mystery to me, but I'm told it happens, so we'll let that slide as well. It appears that if you have decent balance and avoid any potentially murderous spouses, the biggest threat to your health on a cruise ship is the medical center. In reference to medical emergencies on ships, our boy Michael Crye notes, "…it's probably the level of care you would receive in a small town."[33] I agree Mike; it's probably the level of care you would receive in a small town—if that town were in Equatorial Guinea or the Amazon. I know I've already devoted an entire section of this book toward discrediting the medical center of Royal Caribbean, but I feel like if I can discourage just one person from going there I will have made a difference. Save them the trouble and give yourself a pregnancy test before you come, guys too.

---

[33] Cuomo, Cruise Ship Confidential, *20/20*.

# CHAPTER X: XXX

***Lesson I've learned the hard way #158: Don't accept Kit Kat bars from strangers.***

      S ince I have spent a good amount of the first half of this book alluding to precautionary pregnancy tests administered by the medical center, I may as well go ahead and begin to explain why the docs and nurses onboard jump straight to pre-natal conclusions. If you're like 75% of the guests who felt comfortable enough to ask us about our personal lives on a cruise ship, you probably skipped right to this chapter with no regard for any other sections of the book. If the old adage "sex sells" still holds true, and I think it's safe to say it does, then the cruise industry is a goldmine of sexual tall tales whose resources have yet to be tapped. The place is like a floating whorehouse, and not the classy kind of burlesque house that includes a show with your money; I mean like the kind with thick, flashing Christmas lights on the exterior trim no matter what time of the year, where clients typically walk away with a smorgasbord of venereal diseases.

      As you can imagine, there are a limited number of people available to sleep with on a cruise ship—part of the reason employees go for guests, and part of the reason lovers are often "recycled" among crewmembers. If you're from a small town, hell if you've ever visited a small town for more than 20 minutes, it's not difficult to realize that word gets around much quicker than in a place where important things are actually occurring. Now, envision that town being about 1000ft in diameter. Gossip practically breaks the sound barrier. My point being, secrets are virtually unheard of on cruise ships, and it's amazing the kind of stories you pick up after just 15 minutes at the crew bar. Who was sent home because they were pregnant, or needed treatment for syphilis, or was allegedly a sex offender that somehow managed to pass that scrupulous background check that RCI conducts?

After trying to research any kind of statistic for the percentage of crew members walking around with STDs, I quickly came to the conclusion that publicizing that kind of information was most likely a breach in HIPAA. However, ask anybody who has ever worked on a cruise ship if they had, received, or bestowed an STD on somebody else, and I think you'll find the percentages much higher than anyone who leaves their child in RCI's daycare would like to believe. Chlamydia, syphilis, gonorrhea, genital warts, herpes, jock itch, yeast infections, HPV, crabs, genital warts, and a slew of the hepatitis's, a cruise ship doctor has most likely seen them all, plus probably a few that haven't been discovered yet.

While they warn us that sleeping with guests is strictly prohibited for legality issues, the truth may be that they have a moral obligation to keep the multitude of STDs within the confines of the ship. Of course this doesn't always happen. The opportunity for a one-night-stand with an attractive stranger who you will never see again and actually have a legitimate excuse for not being able to contact afterward is all too tempting for some to pass up. Once, I was even asked by a female guest to vouch for a Mexican cruise staffer's "adequacy" in the sack. Apparently my kind recommendation sealed the deal for him later that night. Mom would be proud.

The crewmembers weren't always the guilty party in this situation however. It seemed to be some guests' modus operandi to sleep with an exotic Brazilian without having to complete the tedious burden of actually traveling to Brazil. I don't doubt that a good percentage of these agendas were met with little resistance and it isn't hard to see why. Perhaps it's the serenity of the undulating waves that, when not too nauseating, act like a natural aphrodisiac. Or maybe it has to do with ships' uncoincedental attempt to employ the most attractive people they can find who are willing to settle for $400 a week and all the fish heads you can eat. Or, it might just have to do with the ships' similarities to prison.

The fact that you cannot leave the ship for nearly seven months at a time leaves workers with limited options to satisfy their voracious sexual appetites. And with the cost of a cruise teetering in the hundreds, conjugal visits from lovers left ashore are not nearly as frequent as they might be in the state penitentiary. Just like prison, your options are limited to what is available in your immediate vicinity (unless you're a real Casanova and make really good use of your few hours in the port), but unlike prison, dropping the soap doesn't have to end the same way...necessarily. Women and men are tossed together in tighter quarters than breeding zoo animals, and with an abundance

- 150 -

of pornography being passed around via massive external hard-drives (a ship necessity), even a priest would have a difficult time behaving properly—and no, the irony of priests behaving properly is not wasted on me, but there was a time when that analogy would've meant something.

In the past, cruise ship employment was predominantly male, a fact that caused an unhealthy amount of sexual promiscuity with female guests. Even on *The Love Boat,* Lauren Tewes held the only female role in the cast as the ship's lovable cruise director Julie McCoy. Whereas cruise directors today are meant to "look available but never be available" (a concept that is not always followed to the T), Julie, and the rest of the cast for that matter, are available to anybody and everybody for a quickie on the Lido deck. Times certainly have changed since those days unfortunately, and inappropriate relationships with guests have to be significantly more discreet, at least in front of figures of authority. But fear not voyeuristic crewmembers, you will hear all about any sexual conquests of passengers—and anything else for that matter—in the crew bar…whether or not you want to. Discretion is not a seaman's strong suit.

For instance, everybody knew our cruise director Mark was bitter for most of my contract because a dancer for whom he had specifically requested be transferred to the *Voyager*, refused to sleep with him. Swing and a miss! He was also Canadian, which posed all kinds of complexes and disappointments in bed.[34] Back to the good stuff.

I'm not sure if it was a cultural thing, a ship thing, or a combination, but there were several situations where I was apparently breaking an unwritten rule that says I have to sleep with you after performing a kind act. For instance, on Christmas Eve my friend and I were eating at the ship's Johnny Rockets, a step up from typical mess hall food, but by no means a five star restaurant. The luxury of dining at a different venue comes with a $4.95 price tag for crew and passenger alike. One of the Nicaraguan dishwashers must have seen us through the pots, pans, counter, and everything else designed to shield the dishwashers from view of the general public, and asked our waiter to say hello to us. He also waved and said he would pick up the check as a Christmas present. A seemingly generous gesture for a man neither of us had ever talked to before. But then again, generosity doesn't truly exist on the ship.

It was, as time would disclose, more of an "investment." Later that night I had left the crew bar to write an email, probably about how nice everybody on the ship was or something ironic like that. Then suddenly, who do I see but the kind soul who had bought Bianca and me dinner; I shall call him "Johnny" for the sole reason that I have blacked out everything about the man that I could. I waved hello and gave a polite head nod, which was apparently code for "please come over here and give me a massage."

---

[34] Disclaimer: This is a joke. I have nothing against Canadians and I was in fact, insultingly so, mistaken for a Canadian myself on many occasions.

As the awkward encounter continued, I slowly turned my head back to my email and proceeded to type, assuming he would take the hint and leave. Maybe looking completely uninterested and slightly annoyed means something different in Nicaragua, or perhaps the aroma of onion rings emitting out of my pores was too enticing to pass up. After a very long five minutes of silence and some "more than friendly" massaging, I decided that his monstrous hands could probably last longer than my Internet connection would and got up to leave.

"Well, I think I'm going to bed now. Thanks again for dinner."

"So we go back to my room now?"

"Umm, no I'm going back to my room, and you can go to anybody else's."

"But I don't get it, I buy you dinner, you owe me."

Now, if I may interject here for a second; I've heard of prostitutes working for money, drugs, passports, etc. But I have yet to come across a prostitute, in my vast array of prostitute literature, who puts out for a $5 meal at Johnny Rockets. Even the one-legged Trixy could conjure up a meal at Red Lobster.

"Yeah I know. That's why I said 'thank you.' Have a good night."

Obviously frazzled, Johnny replied disgustedly, "I could've bought my wife a dinner and she would've slept with me."

Wife? Of course he has a wife back home and absolutely no reservations about sharing that information with somebody he was currently trying to sleep with. "Sounds like you kids have something real special. I would hate to cause any rifts in such a solid matrimony."

"What? No she don't know what happens on the ship. It's fine."

"As much as I admire your loyalty to your wife, I'm gonna have to pass."

And with that, I took off at a pace I haven't been capable of since 7th grade gym class when running the 400-meter dash. Johnny's Rocket would have to settle for Tween deck porn tonight.

Encounters like this weren't all that rare either—in fact, they were annoyingly common. I can recall another time shortly after when I was at the slop chest waiting to purchase some toothpaste and the Croatian man in front of me was buying the only thing Croatian men on board ever buy—a Kit Kat bar. As he was about to leave, he saw me waiting behind him and ordered another one, handing it to me as he was on his way out.

"Thanks," I replied to his random act of kindness, nearly convinced that there were a few decent men on the ship. As you can imagine, I could not have been more wrong. I have determined that I am either an incredibly poor judge of character, ridiculously optimistic, or just plain old naïve. I blame Walt Disney.

Later that night, I was doing my daily check-in at the crew bar (it was actually an all crew party that night, so it would've been highly frowned upon had I not been in attendance), and I see the man who bought me the finest chocolate the slop chest had to offer. Eye contact was had by all and this became yet another unintentional sign to come join me while surrounded by friends and with music blasting in the background.

"Hello how are you?" he shouted directly into my ear at a decibel louder than I thought capable by a human voice box

"I'm good. Fun party right?"

"Yeah. Why don't we go back to your cabin?"

Wow, so we're going with the subtle route today I see. "I don't even know you."

"We can get to know each other, or we can go back to my cabin." I know what you're thinking right? He's a regular Casanova, but it *was* a really fun party so my hand was all but forced in the matter.

"How about I go buy you a Kit Kat bar so we never have to have this conversation again?" is what I wanted to respond. Instead, I pretended my wallet was a deck phone and told him that my roommate was a raging alcoholic and needed me to buy her another drink (half true), before skirting off to the other side of the bar. I stopped accepting gifts from strangers after that.

But maybe I'm being too hard on my coworkers. Creeps exist everywhere. I can't say if there's a higher ratio on cruise ships or if it is the culture on board that makes it seem much more acceptable than on dry land. And lord knows there is a dramatically different culture on a ship. Increased freedoms (especially if you hail from a country where sexual repression is a sign of your honor), the idea that nobody from your "real life" will ever find out about it, a population of generally good looking people whose sex drives appear to increase with every passing cruise, and copious amounts of cheap alcohol all play a role in shaping the culture of casual sex on cruise ships.

Some fun stories I heard were of a one Kyle Parker, representing the fine sport staff. While I never had the pleasure of meeting Mr. Parker, his legend lived on through stories passed down both verbally, and those detailed in the written warnings he received and easily viewed by Jason and I on the office computer. It seemed like anytime Jason or I inquired about Kyle somebody who knew him would roll their eyes and smile, picturing one of the crazy anecdotes they associated with him. Ricky, our second supervisor on the contract, complained one day about the "worst sports staff worker he's ever had."

"This guy was always showing up to work drunk and never listened to orders," Ricky said to Jason and me one time.

"Was this guy's name Kyle Parker by chance?" I asked.

"You knew him?"

Jason and I both exchanged looks and laughed.

"Not exactly," we replied in sync.

Then, like children sitting around a campfire and wanting to hear a ghost story, we asked Ricky if he had any stories about Kyle that he was willing to share.

"Of course I do! Dat man's whole life was one giant ridiculous story," he told us in his thick Trinidadian accent. "He would sleep with guests all the time. Mothers, sisters, cousins. I have never seen nobody suck back dat many drinks at da bar neitha. He drinks bottles of wine at a time and he drank dat Red Bull like it was water. I think he probably had a case of it every two days. One time, he was having sex with this spa girl and right der in the da middle of it he had a heart attack right on top of her! She had to get dressed and take him to the medical center."

"How old was he?" Jason and I both inquired.

"Twenty-three!"

"Wow, sounds like he really adopted that carpe diem mentality huh?"

"What's dat?" Ricky would ask, as he did when we used any foreign word that couldn't be learned from watching Dora the Explorer.

I was never able to confirm nor deny such a rumor, mostly in an effort to avoid a really awkward facebook conversation with a man I had never met, but other crewmembers' descriptions of Kyle led me to believe this tragedy was completely plausible. Rest assured, according to his facebook page, Kyle is alive and still employed by Royal Caribbean when this book was started.

Again, while discretion may be the backbone of the cruise industry, it is conspicuously absent in regard to the lives of crewmembers. Every morning shift I had with Jason would begin with him asking, "So did you take anybody back to your cabin last night?" The first couple of days he asked I assumed he was kidding. But as those days turned into weeks, and those weeks turned into months, I realized that

Jason was just a pervert. But an entertaining pervert.

Jason would always have a story for me to help pass the time when Ricky wasn't forcing us to play UNO at the Rockwall. Some were about his life. These included the time he slept with a girl in her cabin and then took all the pills he could from her room the next morning while she lay asleep in her bed. Class act, right? Or the time he sent the South African spa girl home with a "going away present" the night before she debarked. To this day I'm still pretty sure he meant herpes. And then there was the time he slept with the British blackjack dealer who was engaged to Leon, a Peruvian bartender. Jason was a man who knew no shame. He didn't even look uncomfortable when Leon was sent up to the rock wall to help belay during a busy time. Ricky and I couldn't stop laughing at the awkward situation he had setup as the two acted as if Jason hadn't bedded the woman Leon was betrothed to. In other words, Jason was the Stifler of Royal Caribbean.

And then, some of Jason's stories were about other people. Such as the underground gay sex world of which I knew relatively little. Jason was my link to who had slept with whom, or who had used what for things I never thought possible. The gay male dancers and ice skaters were the subject of most of these stories, but Jason also made claims that one of the married production men was actually gay and participating in these activities as well. Or that our first boss Pablo had sex with a woman in the golf simulator until she noticed there was a hole in his penis where he had it pierced earlier.

While I'm not sure how much credibility any of Jason's stories had, they would certainly fetch a solid price in Hollywood…at least its pornography division. Unfortunately for the unassuming characters in many of these stories, the gossip was not relegated to Royal Caribbean employees only. They could be heard in coffee shops, McDonald's, or crew clubs, any haven that provided free or cheap Internet for various cruise ship crewmembers.

Like an incriminating game of telephone, crewmembers from Princess, Carnival, and Norwegian Cruise Lines rehashed erotic stories they had recently heard aboard. For instance, there was a scandal on Princess that involved the spa girls allowing themselves to be videotaped doing things you can imagine a masseuse would do in her personal relationships, but never actually wanted confirmed via tape. The video, as with everything worthy of it, wound up on the Internet and all involved were fired. As I don't recall seeing a clause in my contract regarding said matter, I'm not sure of the technical reasoning behind their firing, but what a way to go out. Tales of patrons receiving "happy endings" from the spa girls was not unheard of either. For an extra, off-the-books fee, male guests could have their tension relieved literally all over their body. They probably would've let you videotape it for an Internet card.

So ship love isn't exactly that which you would find in a Danielle Steele novel, and I say that knowing my grandma will probably no longer purchase this book. But the combination of paint fumes constantly filling the ship, combined with copious amounts of alcohol and the lack of suitors available all tend to lead crewmembers into each other's arms. And you're about as likely to find monogamy on a ship as you are a health inspector. Of course, there is usually one prince among the frogs, but he usually comes to his senses after one contract and moves back across the planet. So the next time you see somebody sanitizing open decks, handrails, hot tubs, or the kid's center, don't think it's only the Nora Virus they're trying to wash away. Chances are, somebody just had sex there.

# CHAPTER XI: THE CREW

*Lesson I've learned the hard way #165:*
*Brazilians on ships are less attractive than they appear.*

By now, I'm sure you have some concept of what many of the employees on the ship were like. And thus far, the vast majority of what I have described has been negative, which absolutely does not represent the majority of the crew on the ship. Of course there were some normal people with whom I have made great efforts to keep touch with, but those folks are much less entertaining. So allow me to describe in greater detail the group of people I worked with on a daily basis.

*Pablo*

Pablo was my first and last boss aboard the *Voyager of the Seas*. He was the one in charge of explaining all the ridiculous rules to me that first week aboard and throughout my tenure, showing me how to falsify my time sheet, and taking me to my emergency muster station so I would know at least where to go (if not what to actually do) for the boat drills. A dark, well built and handsome Brazilian, his exotic external good looks became uglier and uglier the more you got to know him. In fact, after everything we've been through, it pains me to even refer to him as attractive. But what can I say, I was naïve when I joined the ship and Pablo's noxiousness was just another thing I would learn in time.

The array of rules that Pablo was so hell-bent on enforcing was the main reason I can no longer stand the thought of the man. At this point, I still can't determine whether they were indeed RCI rules, or if Pablo made some up in a pathetic sort of power trip. Some of the rules Pablo informed me of could be categorized into levels, and during one slow day at work I attempted to classify them.

### *Annoying Rules:*

\*No open toed shoes are to be worn by crewmembers on the ship, ever. Keep in mind that this would technically mean that when we go to the beach in port, we would have to wear sneakers the 10 yards to the gangway, and then we were free to change into our flip-flops once off the ship. Of course, nobody actually did this, but it's just another reason to dole out a warning. The ship claimed that it is for "our safety." Apparently passengers have toes of steel that exempt them from this rule.

\*No crewmembers should be seen without wearing a nametag. I'm pretty sure this was just to make our lives miserable. Do you make Cletus wear his McDonald's nametag when he's Christmas shopping with his family? It's basically a way to make sure we help passengers even when we're not on the clock and it's annoying as shit.

\*Dress blues or formal wear had to be worn in public areas on respective nights. Some cruise directors were more lenient about this than others. Luckily, my second cruise director allowed us to wear our own smart casual clothing on certain nights, but before him there were no exceptions to having to don my Amish girl outfit. If we wanted to do something other than hang out in our rooms, go to the crew bar or the gym, we had to wear those outlandish dress blues. Formal nights required a ball gown for women, or a tuxedo for men. I actually had to physically tie a black skirt around my legs so my "formal" black dress, which was knee length, would be an appropriate length in guest areas…it looked more seamless than it sounds.

*Shirts must be tucked in at all times. This rule was reasonable enough, if Pablo could understand that wearing a rock wall harness for eight hours a day has the tendency to un-tuck your shirt. He probably didn't notice because his shirts were too tight and short to tuck in, but my colleagues and I took a good amount of flack for it.

*Employees are not allowed to hang out with guests outside of work under any circumstances. Confusing perhaps, as we are supposed to "Deliver the Wow." I could not understand what we were meant to do when guests would come up to us in the Vault to talk. Security would give us dirty looks when they saw us fraternizing with guests, and if we just made an excuse to leave, guests would give us dirty looks and possibly a bad comment card—akin to a crucifixion as an employee on a ship. I saw the look in their eyes when I made excuses to leave; it was the same look I saw in all those creeps at bars who I actually wanted to get away from. It was a look that said, "I'm going to find your car and slash your tires." But in this case, the person in question usually knew exactly where to find you, an unfortunate advantage to them. Most of the time this led to crewmembers taking their chances with security, talking to the guest under the pretense that we "didn't want to be rude." Just another contradiction between policies & procedures that could get you into some hot water if you stepped on the wrong toes.

### *Stupid Rules:*

*Crewmembers are not, under any circumstances, allowed to utilize passenger elevators. The rationale behind this was that there are no cameras on elevators, and if an assault were to take place with a crewmember the company could be liable. What they don't seem to care about is that crew elevators don't have cameras either and an attack is just as likely, if not more so, to take place in one of those. Perhaps they're assuming that, in general, nationals of other countries are less litigious than the American majority of passengers and therefore less likely to sue the company. Or maybe we had signed something in our contract waiving our rights to take any legal action against the company. Regardless of the reasons, waiting for the few crew elevators that worked was only slightly less annoying than waiting for an operable washer or dryer.

*Crewmembers are not allowed to sit down in guest areas. I learned this the hard way when I had the audacity to tie my shoe. A deckhand zoomed over to me as if I had C4 explosives strapped to my body.

"What do you think you're doing?!" he asked.

"Umm what? I...uh...I was just tying my shoe?" Even after the most trivial occurrence, the ship had a way of making you feel like you had just stolen precious medication from children with leukemia.

"Well you're not allowed to sit there."

"Oh, I'm sorry I didn't know. Is there anywhere I can sit?"

"Yeah, the crew bar, now get out of here. You can stand while you tie your shoe, these chairs are for passengers."

"Thanks for the pointer, you have yourself a good night." He mumbled something under his breathe as he left, and when he had his back turned you better believe I sat my ass on that chair and tied my shoe. I can honestly say I have never felt like such a badass for properly affixing my footwear.

I'm not quite sure why we're not allowed to sit in completely vacant guest areas (aside from the theatre if watching a production, but there's a host of other rules associated with that situation). Maybe it's because they don't want passengers to know that they have indeed found a race of super humans who can work 13-hour days for 9 straight months without a single day off and not need to sit down.

*Another stupid rule, void of any and all common sense, is that no crewmembers are allowed to wear shorts in the staff or crew mess, *unless* they are part of your uniform. The rationale for no shorts is that somehow germs from your knees will jump into the food dishes and it's "unsanitary." Here's my take: serving the same fish heads in a vat of butter water for days is unsanitary, wearing shorts does not have to be. And if wearing shorts in the vicinity of food is such an atrocity, why are crew permitted to wear uniform shorts? Are your legs not as bacteria laden while wearing company shorts? Because in my experience, the opposite is true. The fact that we were in the Caribbean with frequently poor ventilation in the crew areas probably posed more of a concern to employee health than exposed shins.

*Crewmembers' rooms are inspected every week during the boat drill. The room was meant to be kept tidy, the beds had to be made, the sink had to be empty, the refrigerator had to be empty, no contraband such as hairdryers, curling irons, or straighteners were allowed, and more. All told, there was an entire page of things that you could get marked down for. Yes, I said marked down— as in, we were graded on our cabin inspections. If you missed enough of the items on the checklist, or if the person inspecting your room was a real asshole, you would receive a cabin failure notice. Three of these notices led to a warning. When I first learned of these cabin inspections, my first reaction was confusion.

"But some of these crew members are in their 50s. You mean to tell me they get in trouble if they don't make their bed?" I asked Pablo.

"Yes. This is a ship, we need discipline here or the whole operation will be chaos."

"One could say the same thing for a coed dorm but nobody checks rooms there."

"Well that's the way things work here, so get used to it."

And I have to say, although some of the losers who graded our room were harsher than inspectors looking for candy at a fat camp, my roommate and I managed to pass 15 of the 16 cabin inspections I was there for. And when we failed, boy did we *fail*. In our hung-over state, we had completely forgotten about cabin inspections as we rushed to get to our muster stations early in the morning. The previous night we had entertained more people than I thought could possibly fit in such a small space. There were drinks everywhere, an Irish tin whistle that seemed to appear out of thin air, guitar strings had been ripped off of my guitar, trash cans were tipped over spilling their contents onto the floor, a half eaten sandwich was sitting out, a painting that had been defaced by my very mature and witty friends was visible for all authority figures to see, and pillows were all over the floor. In short, it looked like a frat house the morning after a mixer. We hadn't made our best effort to clean, but it had been one hell of a night. This would be confirmed by the fact that four other rooms in our hallway also failed cabin inspection that morning.

### *Ridiculous Rules:*

*Crewmembers are not allowed to sit more than four to a table when eating in the Windjammer. If we were willing to pay $3, and were wearing appropriate clothing and nametags, we were allowed to eat in this passenger buffet. If there were five of us however, we were not permitted to sit together. We would have to break such a rowdy group into two separate tables. Again, I'm not sure what the rationale for this was. Maybe we were too big of a presence and became an intimidating machine when we sat five to a table. Although I'm not sure how much of a difference was made when we sat one foot apart, but the Policies & Procedures weren't all that well thought out.

*Crewmembers are not allowed to eat or drink in front of guests (with the exception of the Windjammer or Portofino's whereby a guest may be allowed to "catch" a crewmember eating). I learned this rule in several different segments. First, we *are* allowed to purchase coffees, teas, or ice cream from a shop in the promenade which is fraught with guests, but we are *not* allowed to drink or eat them in public view. After I had just purchased a tea, I learned this rule the way I learned so many others.

"What do you think you're doing?" Pablo questioned when he saw me carrying my tea.

"What do you mean? Am I supposed to be at work right now I checked the schedule and..."

"No! I mean with that drink, you're not allowed to drink it!" Pablo cut me off.

"Then why the hell did they just let me pay $3.75 for it?"

"I mean you're not allowed to drink it *here*. You can't drink in passenger areas."

"Even tea?" I asked.

"Even water!" Pablo retorted.

To say Pablo was a stickler for these stupid rules would be an understatement. He was the type of person who took his job so seriously you would think there were lives at stake. If he were a policeman he wouldn't speed. Of course, when it came to important aspects of the job, say, not lying on our time sheets, he actually demanded that we not follow the rules. And then there was that time he reportedly had sex in the golf simulator, but that was before he was given the power associated with a managerial position. And with great power comes great abuse of that power.

A few weeks had passed and I had decided to purchase another chai tea. This time, I didn't dare take a sip of it until I reached a crew area, but evidently that wasn't enough. I felt Pablo lurking behind me and, seeing as how I was actually following the rules I didn't feel it necessary to pretend I didn't see him and hustle out of there.

"Hey boss how's it going?"

"I thought I told you, you can't drink in passenger areas," Pablo said sternly.

"But...what? I didn't...I mean, I haven't taken a sip."

Sensing that maybe I was in the right here, I'm pretty sure Pablo made up another rule on the spot to save face.

"You can't carry it like that." (I had been carrying it with my palm cupped around the side, as a human with functioning, non-deformed hands would typically carry a drink). "You need to carry it like this." And Pablo took my cup and held it on the top with his hand covering the lid.

"You've got to be kidding me. There is no way that that rule is in the SQM manual," I was thinking to myself. Then again, I'd never actually been given or even seen a copy of this hilarious rulebook, so maybe it was. There had been other specific, seemingly ridiculous rules in the manual such as a list of words crewmembers are not allowed to use. If you're thinking I'm going to explain why you cannot use them, don't hold your breath. I have no idea. Some of the words we weren't allowed to use included, "excellent," "passenger," or "cabin," to name a few. I'm pretty sure the people in charge of "brand quality" were trying to convince their superiors that their jobs were still necessary. I would love to sit in on that meeting:

"Okay, so what have you guys been doing for the past week?"

"Well, um, we…uh…we have come to the conclusion that it would help business if…um…if we prohibited certain words from being used on the ship…umm, yea, that's it."

"Really? What words did you have in mind?"

"Uhhh…hmmm…well right now we've determined that "cabin" shouldn't be used. It's umm, it uh...reminds people that they're on a ship. We should use "staterooms" instead. And like I said, our surveys are finding all kinds of words that are less than ideal to use. We'll have to continue to research this sir."

"I like it. Good work Bruce."

These are the things I contemplated while I melted in the 105 degree Bahamian sun, unable to drink water for four hours straight.

*Crewmembers are prohibited from putting their hands in their pockets. Maybe this looks unprofessional, or maybe the company is afraid somebody will pull a shank out of their pockets, I'm not sure. What I am sure of, is that when you are standing on Deck 17 at 8 p.m. on a day that it had just snowed in Texas, our t-shirts, light warm-up jacket and pants are not nearly warm enough. Does the company issue gloves? No. Does that give you the right to put your hands in your pockets? Of course not. And don't you dare try to blame standing out in the cold for hours without appropriate clothing for getting you sick. The medical center knows why you got sick, it's because you didn't wash your hands enough. Did you know that washing your hands can also reverse pregnancy? Because according to the medical center, that's a possibility. I could go on and on with these rules, but this chapter is meant to be about my comrades in dress blues, so I'll get back to that.

Pablo was a tough read from the start. I had known him all of 48 hours before he was lamenting to me about his difficult upbringing in Brazil. He had evidently fallen into a rough crowd in São Paulo and joined a semi-gang whose biggest accomplishment was trying eight different drugs in a week. He was an "incredible" soccer player who could have gone pro if a brain sat in the space between his ears...I mean if he hadn't blown out his knee. This setback undoubtedly led to more drug use, and his sister, seeing his life spiraling out of control, encouraged him to apply for work on a cruise ship. Probably after hearing about his illustrious soccer career, Royal Caribbean hired him as a member of their elite sport staff.

"Ships saved my life," he would recall, with the water level in his eyes reaching heights dangerously close to making this a very uncomfortable situation. "If it weren't for ships I would be dead." Well Royal Caribbean, it sounds like you found yourself a new poster boy for the next time a courtroom tries to pin an unlawful death lawsuit on you.

"There were a couple times in college that I'm pretty sure I should have had my stomach pumped," is all I could muster, trying to break the awkward silence and offer something slightly personal to this complete stranger. I probably could've done better had I dug deeper, but I was caught a little off guard with my new role as priest in a confessional.

A role, might I add, that quickly dissipated when Pablo mentioned that his fiancé was joining the ship in a couple of weeks so unfortunately there was "no chance for us." I'm not sure if he was kidding or not, but I laughed regardless.

"Damn," I lamented as I snapped my fingers in disappointment. "What's her name? How long have you two been dating for?"

"Her name is Kristy. She's a South African spa girl."

If you haven't noticed already, everybody on a ship is identified by their ethnicity and department.

"We met at the crew bar about four months ago. She came up to me and asked me why I hadn't asked her out yet. Then we went out (which I took to mean they ventured to the crew bar together as opposed to meeting there) and she went on vacation right after I proposed to her."

"Wow, and she's been gone for a couple of months? So you guys were only together on the ship for a couple of months before getting engaged?"

"Well, we actually broke up a couple of times during that time, but we're back together now. When you know, you know. You know?"

I hope he didn't take the skeptical look on my face to imply that this was unusual. Surely there are people who get married in Vegas who have known each other for a shorter period of time. If Britney Spears can make that mistake, then why can't Pablo? A few weeks before she was to arrive, Kristy sent Pablo a bouquet of red roses as a "gesture of her love."

"Do you think she's trying to make him look gay so other girls stay away from him?" Jason asked me.

"I think she should've sent pink roses for that, but who knows."

If that had been her intention, it worked better than anybody could've imagined. Pablo took his roses with him to work so they could get sunlight, as if the sun would miraculously revive flowers that had been dying since they were cut over a week ago. In truth, the wind exposure they received on deck 17 probably ended up shortening their lives. But Pablo spent hours watching them, making sure they were placed in the safest area of the skating track. I didn't want to break the news to him that the only way those flowers wouldn't be rotting away when Kristy got here weeks later is if he froze them, plus it was rather humorous watching him treat this flora better than he treated us.

If you can't already tell, Pablo liked to make a big deal about trivial issues. If the sliding glass door to the skate shop was not 100% open he would threaten to give you a warning. If he saw us in our day uniforms 10 minutes after we were supposed to be in our evening uniforms he would tell us to go change, and reassure us that we were lucky it was he who had caught us first, and not the cruise director. If we let one guest climb the rock wall one minute after we were meant to have closed, he would launch into an in-depth lecture about how a group of sixty Japanese tourists came right before he closed one time, and if he had let one go he would've had to let them all go.

"But Pablo, there's not sixty Japanese tourists in sight," I would clarify.

"It doesn't matter! They could come up and see that boy climbing and want to climb."

"Can't we just say we're closed? Since we will be when he gets down?"

"It doesn't work like that," he would scoff, as if I had just suggested the most asinine thing he had ever heard, and walked away after rolling his eyes in disgust.

I guess Pablo was in no mood to finish this conversation, but I was curious to figure out how things worked on the ship. Eventually, I would come to learn a general formula for how things worked. Take an idea or method that makes the most logical sense, find the complete opposite of that, and the way RCI does things is strikingly similar to that approach. Not the most scientific, and it lends itself to ideas you never thought possible in a business operating in the 21st century, but it did curb the surprise at such ignorance. I also learned to take the same approach with Pablo, which is probably the only way I could handle being managed by him for as long as I was.

*Jason*

I'm not sure what kind of impression I've given the reader about Jason through his previous exposure in the book, but rest assured, it is all true. In case you've forgotten, Jason was my British coworker at the rock wall and primary form of daily entertainment. This was Jason's third contract on RCI. He'd worked training sled dogs in Lapland, managed to pick up two arrests in

England: one for climbing a flagpole and throwing a beer bottle at a crowd, and one for getting into a fight—both after a soccer game. He'd worked construction in Australia for years and was a fitness instructor for another cruise ship. It seemed that he had so many life experiences that it led me to question just how old Jason was (27 at the time).

He had dirty blonde, spiked hair, which he would later trade in for a shaved head halfway through his contract. What he lacked in height (about 5'8") he made up for in musculature. He also claimed to have played professional soccer, and watching Pablo and him duke it out on the sports court was like watching gladiators fight to the death. Jason spoke with a thick Cockney accent, the kind where he would say, "firty free" in reference to the number 33. Most Brits considered this a sign of poor education, but I found it charming.

A perpetual gossip, Jason was my backup informant of who's sleeping with who when I didn't see it for myself. Of course, a lot of the time it was just him telling me about which spa girl he'd brought back to his cabin that night—always with his roommate present might I add. There was the time Jason slept with Cara, a British spa girl, when he knew that Riley, an Australian youth staff, had slept with her the night before and had a considerable crush on her. Watching this whole ordeal unfold was like watching a bad episode of *Gossip Girl*, where the conniving bitch was a guy. Jason wasn't the only one who had claws though.

In an episode I call "The Katie-Riley-Jason Love Triangle," Riley gets the last laugh when he managed to bed the 18-year-old dancer from Texas on multiple occasions. Jason had been publicly courting her, as much as Jason has probably ever "courted" a girl—i.e. buying her drinks and talking to her. Everybody benefited from Jason's newfound happiness at back deck. He gave me his crew card to buy a six-pack of Smirnoff Ice for Katie and so graciously told me that I could get a drink on him as well. So naturally, I ordered as many drinks as I could physically carry, along with drinks for everybody sitting at the bar, and handed Jason his liquid aphrodisiac.

After Katie and Jason spent the night drinking and flirting, she ended up leaving with Riley while Jason was "in the loo." I'm not sure if Jason was more upset about the fact that Katie left with Riley or that his $6 investment of drinks had not panned out. Either way, this saga would reach its boiling point later in the highly anticipated season finale that you'll have to stay tuned for.

What's a bit stranger about this love triangle, and another reason it was a television worthy drama, was that Riley and Jason seemed to be each other's best friend on the ship. They would get off the ship together in port, watch movies, and throw back beers like nothing had ever happened after they both vied for the love of the same teenage girl. I questioned their relationship once and Jason assured me that "It's a ship, girls have to get recycled. There are no hard feelings." And there you have it. Another brief, yet accurate synopsis of ship love.

When I first joined the ship, Pablo had advised me not to take after Jason's work ethic. Juan, his Brazilian golden boy, was a much better model to learn from. I guess coming to work smelling like rum and corn chips hadn't earned Jason "Employee of the Month" just yet. Chances were looking even slimmer after a particular rendezvous with Cara and Riley in the Bahamas.

The trio had gone to the beach one day with the intention of procuring some of the island's most popular herb. Unfortunately for them, the shady, homeless type man only had cocaine available that day.

"Many tourists come the past few days, I got none of that Mary Jane left brotha. But I'll give you 'dis at a discount since it's not really what you want. You ain't cops are you?"

I laughed at the thought of anybody mistaking Jason for a man of the law, but the story gets better. As the three crewmembers snorted the "true white gold" as Jason called it, they realized the ship was about to take off without them. In their haste to get back to the ship, they had completely forgotten that they still had a bag of coke in Riley's pocket. Luckily for them, the inadequacy of RCI's security forces allowed me to see them again on Deck 17 as opposed to on *Locked Up Abroad*. Jason had changed into his uniform and managed to show up to work only ten minutes late. Granted, he reeked of alcohol, had sand caked all over his face, and a generally disheveled appearance, but hey, he wasn't going for employee of the month. His disorientation drew the attention of Pablo, who simply told him to go shower and come back to the rock wall. About an hour later, Jason returned looking just as confused, but smelling slightly more sober.

"Jason, you still have sand on the back of your neck, did you take a shower?" I asked.

"No. Once I got to my room I splashed water on my hair and face and called Riley and Cara and we finished off the rest of the cocaine. Riley was whining about how he didn't want to get caught with it. Guess he didn't want to spend time in a Bahamian jail or something, I don't know. I don't know what's going on. But the coke is gone, so we can't offer you any."

"Damn. When I joined this ship I was really hoping to cross 'Use hard drugs that I acquired from a hobo in a third world country' off my bucket list. I guess there's always Jamaica."

Jason managed to finish the shift under Pablo's skeptical eyes without dropping any kids from the rock wall, and then headed to the bar.

This little anecdote, combined with Pablo's perpetual criticisms, is why I found it awfully confusing when Pablo nominated Jason for an employment award. Especially since there were two perfectly competent employees of his who hadn't snorted coke before and during work, a time that he was meant to be showering off his drunkenness.

"Pablo, I thought you hated Jason? You're always telling me not to follow his example. Why would you nominate him for a service award?"

"He did a good job hosting the Royal Olympics on the crossing. Why are you out to destroy him?"

"Out to destroy him? I'm the only one who likes the way Jason does things around here," I thought to myself. And who talks like that anyway? What was this, *Star Wars*?

"I'm not trying to *destroy* anybody Pablo. I just find it odd that you would publicly denounce his work ethic, and then give him an award stating the complete opposite." It makes me feel like I should come into work drunk more often, I felt like adding.

"Well he's obviously taking his job more seriously these days."

This was about four days after the illicit drug ordeal.

"Obviously," I responded, not wanting to get Jason in trouble...or arrested. "Can I use Jason as an example now?"

He just smirked his creepy smirk, as he always did when he didn't want to answer a question, and we both looked over at Jason. He was sleeping on the desk of the skate shop. God bless him.

*Juan*

Juan, along with Jason, was the other member of the sport staff when I first joined the crew, as well as my first friend on the ship. Also an attractive Brazilian, Juan was fluent in five languages, very personable and actually read books in his spare time. A rare find on a cruise ship! When Juan told me about *his* journey to board the ship, it made my debacle sound like a cakewalk. I was fortunate enough to not have to take a taxi into a different country at least. Juan was dating a German spa girl he had met on the ship on a previous contract and hadn't seen in months. Coming from a man who maintains that the "greatest day of his life" was when he was denied the opportunity to give blood because he'd had too many sexual partners, this time of celibacy was a rough time for him.

Apparently tequila is the best medicine for loneliness. I had thought six years in post secondary education had sufficiently prepared me for senseless binge drinking, but working on a cruise ship redefines the word "alcoholic." Straight shots at any and all hours of the day were a prerequisite to surviving onboard, and if you couldn't handle it you would get left behind. It was like some sort of bizarro Noah's ark, where only the immoral people made the cut. Sure makes me want to attend Carnival in Rio before the liver damage sets in.

Juan left us after one short month, before reaching the Caribbean and therefore didn't have the opportunity to return to the ship on hard drugs as Jason did, so I'm going to go ahead and rap this section up.

*Bianca*

Bianca was yet another Brazilian sport staffer who came on to replace Juan about a month after my contract had started. Working on contract numero cinco, Bianca was one of the many crewmembers who was hoping to find Mr. Right aboard the *Voyager of the Seas*. She had come close a couple of times, but neither of her engagements actually made it to the altar. Bianca took the expression, "you've got to kiss a lot of frogs before you can find your prince," to heart. Except she replaced "frogs" with "any crewmember with at least half a stripe," and "kiss" with "sleep with."

Bianca was Pablo's favorite sport staff, mainly because she was Brazilian, but also because she was subordinate. He loved how she closed the rock wall on time, making sure 60 Japanese tourists wouldn't get the best of us. He loved how she never challenged him on any of the stupid shit he said or did. And it probably didn't hurt that she had enormous tits. We're talking cantaloupe sized knockers on an otherwise normally proportioned body. This, combined with the fact that she was searching for a mate like a cat in heat made her awfully desirable to any man looking to get laid.

So I'm sure it came as a huge blow to her self-esteem to get denied by Jason. Watching her proposition herself to him while working wouldn't have been as embarrassing if the world's biggest horn dog had obliged. To her credit, she was able to bed several respectable crewmembers. An attractive British guitarist, multiple guest entertainers who specialized in flexibility, an Argentinean saxophone player, and a suave Brazilian cruise staffer to name a few. She also had a porn collection that rivaled that of Roman Polanski. But when Bianca wasn't trying to find a suitor, she was a friendly and welcoming coworker who I was glad to have onboard.

*Ricky*

My Trinidadian fill-in boss and oftentimes sexual harasser, Ricky was a breath of fresh air from the regime that Pablo had us living under. He was a large black man with a shaved head, who couldn't swim and would rather burn one down than work. He spoke with a thick island accent that made me feel like I was in a living sequel to *Cool Runnings*—a less inspirational, highly disappointing sequel, but a sequel nonetheless.

Jason, who wasn't exactly Mr. P.C., had a new and insulting name for him every time he spoke about him to me, none of which I feel comfortable enough to include in a book that my friends have assured me at least 28 people will read.

The first day I had the pleasure of meeting Ricky, he seemed like a big lovable fool who would provide Jason and me with limitless entertainment. We were all working on the sports deck when, at approximately 5 p.m., Ricky informed me that he had to go "take care of some paperwork" for a little bit and left Jason and me at the rock wall; Bianca was at the skating track at the time. An hour and a half had passed when Jason finally asked,

"Where's Ricky gone?" in his delightful British accent.

"He said he was going to do paperwork and would be back soon. I don't know if he knows that we close in 25 minutes," I responded.

All of a sudden the phone rang at the rock wall desk. It was Bianca.

"Where the hell is Ricky?! These guests are asking to speak to my manager because they have a handicapped boy who wants to roll around the skating track, but I say he no can."

"Bianca, nobody is on the track, nobody has been on the track in over an hour, just let him wheel around for 10 minutes. I think Ricky fell overboard," I responded.

"But it's a liability!" This, I should mention, was Bianca's favorite American saying. I heard it at least twice a day.

"Crshsshshh, what's that Bianca? I'm sorry I can't hear you, I think there's a bad connection," I shouted as I crumpled more rock wall disclaimer paper into the receiver.

"What are you doing to the phone? You know I can see you right?"

"Well no actually, I was under the impression that you were near-sighted, but listen I'm gonna go get some water from the bar, and listen, it'll probably be a bigger liability if you prohibit that kid from going on the skating track because he's handicapped than if you let him in. I'll send Ricky down if he ever comes back."

As I went through the emergency exit in the card room—our shortcut to the bar—I was slightly alarmed to see my new boss sitting at the bar. Concerned that he would find me away from the rock wall for one minute, an offense that would've landed me a scolding from Pablo, I stammered over my words for a few seconds.

"Oh hey, uh, Ricky, umm, what's going on? I just came in to grab a glass of water real quick, I'll get back in a…" and then it hit me. Why was I defending myself here? I had a legitimate reason to be at the bar. Apparently Ricky's "office" was the bar, and his "paperwork" was a strawberry daiquiri.

"Come on in girl, have a seat!"

I did, partly because he was my boss, and partly because he sounded like a combination of Sebastian from *The Little Mermaid* and Rafiki from *The Lion King*, and I thought it would be a fun conversation. Fun, it was not; but entertaining, absolutely. Ricky had been talking to the bartender, an unsuspecting young man from Nicaragua, about selling subwoofers.

"Mon, you would not believe da sound system on my car. Ladies here me comin from a mile away."

"At least he gives them fair warning," I thought to myself…at least I think it was to myself. He seemed unfazed regardless.

"I know a guy who can get them sent to your home dirt cheap. DIRT CHEAP mon!"

"I don't know Ricky, I feel like my car isn't worth enough to invest in subwoofers. It don't even have a CD player," the bartender responded.

"Dat's okay mon, I can get you dat too, and external hard drives, you need any of 'dem? I got loads of dem for sale."

Here Ricky was, his first day on the *Voyager*, trying to sell what probably amounted to stolen electronics to complete strangers. Oh yes,

- 185 -

things were going to get much better for us. We weren't in Kansas anymore Jason—Kansas of course being hell on earth.

As the conversation was wrapping up, Jason entered the bar to find us all sitting there talking. Now there was nobody at the wall. Pablo had been known to give people warnings for much less, but all Ricky said was, "Dis is a virgin daiquiri," in an effort to defend the fact that he was drinking on duty. Sure it was Ricky. Jason and I exchanged looks and tried to conceal our smiles. As we all got up to leave, Ricky looked at the poor bartender and said, "You ain't gonna charge me for dis right mon?" I use that question mark liberally, as I'm still not sure if it was a question or a statement the way he said it. And there it was. In the first day alone, Ricky had:

1. Drank on the job
2. Skipped work to drink on the job
3. Tried to sell stolen goods to somebody who had no use for them
4. Bullied a bartender into not charging him for drinks
5. Inspired us all.

When we returned to the rock wall Bianca was frantically calling again. I couldn't hear what she said, but I did hear Ricky's part of the conversation.

"Whaddaya mean? Why can't he walk? How did he get on dis ship if he can't walk? ... So does he want to put skates on his feet or just roll around the track?...How is dat different den what he does everyday?... I guess if he wants to he can, and Bianca? Ask him if he needs a new hard drive, I can get him a good deal."

Ever the entrepreneur, Ricky would see an opportunity, nay, what he *thought* was an opportunity, and try to capitalize on it. Dennis, the man in charge of lighting for the production shows reminisced about an older ship he and Ricky were on together.

"I was moving speakers from the theater to another room and Ricky was on the elevator with me. He flat out asked me if he could have the speakers. He said they looked old and Royal Caribbean shouldn't use them. Then he offered to take them for me. At first I laughed, but then I realized he was serious."

And then there was Ricky the DJ. Bianca had heard some of the music he played one night at the crew bar and inquired if he could put some songs on her computer. Being the gentleman that Ricky was, he not only put on countless songs, but also his entire porn collection, which he aptly titled, *Bianca's Special*. Unbeknownst to herself, Bianca opened this folder in the crew bar with several people around, eager to know what it was. No cleverly labeled porn films like *Jamaican Me Horny*, or *Saving Ryan's Privates*, or even *Florence of the Labia*. Just some hard-core animal porn titled *On a German Farm* with special effects from the '80s. I guess some things are timeless. I know personally I will never be able to forget some of those images…as hard as I try.

*Diego*
        I wish that I could say what struck me first about Diego was the way his pensive eyes acted as a gateway to his deeply profound soul. Or, that his strapping good looks and quixotic elocution were enough to make even the strongest of women fall. But those would both be lies; it was his height. Definitely his height. Diego, one of many Mexican youth staffers (seriously they could've fielded a soccer team), probably rang in at about 5'8"—in heels. For better or worse, he didn't wear heels often, save the time he had to enter the men's sexy legs competition. I don't consider myself *incredibly* shallow, but I would be lying if I said I didn't have any hesitations about dating someone who doesn't tower over me. I'm going to go ahead and assume it's evolution's fault where the males are meant to protect the females while the females do pretty much everything else. Then I remembered this was the 21st century and my chances of being attacked by a gorilla in the middle of the ocean were *much* lower, gorillas don't like water.
        Diego also happened to be one of the very few male staff members who didn't blatantly sexually harass me, or secretly put my keycard next to his phone so the magnetic strip wouldn't work and I would have to spend the night in his room (not unheard of, unfortunately). How could I resist?
        For those curious, dating on a cruise ship is a little different than on land. Mainly in the fact that it doesn't exist. You are either married to somebody or sleeping with them, and chances are

they are still married, just not to you. It's hard to date when you are working a combined 24 hours a day. If you're lucky, you will both have lunch off at the same time and get to sit at the same table in the mess hall. There, you can judge your friend based on his food choices or breathe a sigh of relief, based on whether he goes for three-day-old fish heads or…anything else. If he is lactose intolerant and continues to go for the daily soft serve ice cream machine, you will count your blessings that you don't work in the same area. On port days, you may be able to debark the ship together, work schedules permitting. Many-a-time lovers will be separated when one of them finds out they are scheduled for port manning that day (meaning they cannot leave the ship),[35] and there is a very small chance the other will stay on the ship when given the opportunity to not stay on the ship.

Anyway, back to Diego. He was short, dark and handsome, not a creep, and not too shabby at dodgeball—a turn on for everybody, am I right ladies? It's hard to pinpoint exactly when Diego fell in love with me. He was impressed with both my ping pong play, and my ability to rebound and exercise after a long night of drinking—and by exercise, I mean play ping pong. He had even asked me if I took up the game to work on my

---

[35] Still not 100% sure of the purpose of this. Possibly so there are enough crewmembers aboard the ship to fend off an attack, or something to that effect. I'm told you are supposed to know when you're scheduled for port manning but I typically saw that news delivered to staff like a slap in the face as they tried to leave.

reflexes for karate, to which I obviously laughed. I would later find out that that is the exact reason he took it up, so this relationship was off to a great start.[36]

When he found out that I played guitar he demanded we go back to my room and write a song. The song was called, "Gato," or, "Cat" in the mother tongue. Needless to say, it was pretty life changing. I can't recall any of the other words, I'm actually pretty sure there were no other words, but at the time (3 a.m.), the wine made it seem Grammy worthy. I can neither confirm nor deny if my neighbors in the rest of the hallway felt this way.

There was one particularly fun day that I was able to get off the ship with Diego. We were in Cozumel and decided to rent scooters and a jeep with a few other friends. Though the speedometers didn't work,[37] we were both fortunate enough to receive the last two helmets. After recklessly swerving through the roads (scooters did not include lessons), we made it to a fun bar/restaurant/water park. I use the term "Water Park" loosely, as it was really just an ocean trampoline, slide, and a few other obstacle-course-like inflatables thrown into the Atlantic. The restaurant permitted free use of the ocean if you were dining with them, but use of the inflatables came with an extra $30 price tag. Scoffing at such

---

[36] His extreme (and probably unnecessary) focus and catlike reflexes combined with his love of karate led to my obvious nickname for him, Mr. Miyagi.

[37] Well, mine didn't work; Diego's was covered with a *Sesame Street* sticker, presumably because it didn't work.

a steep fee, we were content to just swim in the ocean—emphasis on the *were.*

After swimming and eating, we heard a loud cowbell ringing, signifying that shot specials were about to commence. Suckers for a good deal, Diego and I challenged each other to partake in their "mystery shot" competition. It involved drinking—and holding down—a combination of whatever bottom shelf liquor and old mixers they were trying to get rid of at the time. Looking back on this years later, I cannot justify my decision to participate in said competition other than foolish pride. The shot tasted like gasoline mixed with coffee grinds. Expired coffee grinds. And I *certainly* cannot justify drinking two of them, other than the fact that it was buy one get one free. Why Diego and I didn't just split two is beyond me.

The combination of these shots, and the noticeable increase in people seemingly having a grand old time on the inflatables made the obstacle course look more and more appealing to us. What remained unappealing was the price. We formulated a plan. Our friends would cause a mild scene to distract the kayaking inflatable fee enforcers, and Diego and I would race through the obstacle course, which we estimated would take under 15 seconds. We signaled our friends, whose "diversion" involved splashing water and screaming—like almost everybody else in the water. Needless to say, it held the kayakers attention for maybe two seconds. Our other estimates were not exactly spot on either. I'm not sure if anybody has had the pleasure of trying an inflatable obstacle course in the ocean, but they are *damn* hard. It probably took us 15 seconds to get up to the starting line. We both fell off into the ocean almost immediately after. I blame the shots.

Our various miscalculations led to the kayaking enforcers to paddle over to us and demand $30. After we pretended we were Russian and didn't understand,[38] they followed us to shore and continued to demand $30 for a mere 15 seconds on their precious (and I'll admit really fun) obstacle course. When they mentioned that they had called the police, Diego and I looked at each other and, as if reading each other's mind, booked it to the scooters.

After we made our getaway, I realized all of the keys must work in all of the scooters because I was certainly not on the scooter I had driven there—the speedometer actually worked on this one.[39]

I don't actually think they called the police on us, but the adrenaline rush and right to call ourselves international criminals[40] was a very bonding experience. While Diego was a great part of my ship life, his stories aren't nearly as entertaining to read about as Elise's.

---

[38] A strategy that works on so many occasions.

[39] After we realized this fun fact we played a game called "move your friend's parked rental scooter a block away and see if they can find it before the ship takes off."

[40] I risk extradition just telling you about this.

*Elise*

I can't help but smile when I look back on any of the memories I have of my fourth/last/best Australian roommate, Elise. Freshly 21, I could never understand how she could drink to excess on a regular basis, often blacking out, and still suffer minimal damage the following morning. And then I realized the legal drinking age in Australia is 18, which means she probably started at about 12. Drinks like a fish, laid back, and an avid hunter of crocodiles, Elise fit the Australian stereotype to a tee. Okay, she didn't actually hunt crocodiles, but she ate that repulsive Vegemite like nobody's business, and call it poetic license but the croc hunting sounded cooler than consuming yeast extract.

The only information I had been given about Elise was that she was a cruise staffer from Australia and a lesbian. Odd I thought, because the first time I saw her she was in the crew bar, three sheets to the wind, making out with the lead guitarist of the ship's band. And Mitch might not be the most masculine man, but I was fairly certain one could tell his gender even through the thickest of beer goggles. As bad as I feel exploiting Elise's sexual endeavors for the public's benefit, her stories are too entertaining to remain untold...plus, I may or may not have changed her name for the book. I also reasoned that anybody prominently donning herself in a toga made of bingo cards isn't all that concerned with candor.

My favorite memory of my favorite roommate probably took place around her third week on the ship. It was 70s night on the ship, which meant the cruise staff (and unfortunately Jason) revisited the decade by dressing up and dancing to classics such as *YMCA* and *It's Raining Men*. It also meant that the cruise staff needed to commence drinking a little earlier than everybody else. After the embarrassment that was 70s night had finished, Elise returned to our room to find that it had been chosen as the designated party room of the night/week/contract—for the record, we were given neither veto power nor votes in this decision.

I'm not sure if Elise had forgotten she'd already consumed 6 shots before 70s night, or if she had remembered the embarrassment to which she just exposed herself, but either way, she busted in as if she were choking on a family of worms and José Cuervo was the only man who could save her.

Details of the night are a little hazy. We did make it up to the bar, partaking in a photo shoot dressed as Rambo draped in toilet paper, consumed a few more drinks, executed a few very graceful cartwheels on the dance floor, sang at least one clichéd karaoke song, and had another conversation about jumping off the back of the ship before Elise was "escorted" back to our room by two of our friends. Either ten minutes or two hours later (like I said my memories from that night were hazy at best), my group of friends decided we should call it a night before the talk of jumping ship led to action.

As we staggered through the "back roads" of the first floor, so as not to tip off security that half of the ship's crew has illegally consumed more than the allotted "one drink per hour" and would certainly not be able to perform their emergency duties should anything happen, we made it back to my cabin in about 10 minutes (about 3 times as long as usual due to the serpentine nature of our gait). While most of us were out in the hall trying to fix priceless artwork that Jason had knocked over, Riley realized he had forgotten his flash drive in our room while he was bringing Elise back and asked for my keys.

About two minutes later he hands me my keys with a face redder than the guests who forget to bring sunscreen to the Caribbean.

"What's wrong with you?" I ask him.

"Umm...can you get my flash drive? I don't think I should go in there right now." Half confused and half annoyed that I was being taken away from the party, I opened my door to find Elise passed out on the floor outside our bathroom, which was coincidentally the same floor next to my bed, our TV, all the furniture, and my guitar. It was a small room. Luckily, I didn't see any blood. It looked as though she had mastered the art of passing out in tight spaces, a skill that she had no doubt picked up at her university. Oh right, and the reason that Riley was blushing—the only time I've EVER seen Riley blush might I add—was most likely due to the fact that Elise was buck naked from the waist down.

As a CPR and First Aid certified employee, I *know* the first thing the Red Cross instructs you to do when presented with such a situation is not to laugh, but I couldn't help myself. Here was this girl who I barely knew, who felt comfortable enough to pass out without any pants on surrounded by empty wine bottles and garbage. I was touched. She looked like one of the petrified corpses that Mount Vesuvius is renowned for, only with more flesh and hair. It wasn't so funny when I realized that it was my room and I would have to clean it up, but I wouldn't come to *that* conclusion for hours. I decided it would be best to call some troops for reinforcement.

"Jennifer! I need your help in here!" I screamed to the other Australian cruise staffer.

"Oh. My. God. What the hell happened in here?! It looks like a train came through and ran over Elise while she was taking a shower."

*Pretty accurate description*, I thought to myself. I threw a gardener's glove that I had obtained at some point in the night over her more...er...sensitive area, and we tried to find some pants to drape over the rest of her body. Unfortunately, it was the blind leading the severely blind that night, and scrambling to clothe our friend with a large crowd of people watching from the hall added pressure to the embarrassing situation.

Now you might be thinking that we should take our dear friend to the closest thing the ship has to a hospital at this point, which would be a reasonable idea on land. However, assuming this wasn't the work of one glass of wine, Elise would most definitely have more than the allotted .08 blood alcohol level running through her veins. And blowing a .09 was immediate grounds for dismissal. We made the educated gamble that her youth would give her an edge in the situation and she'd be fine. Besides, as I mentioned earlier the medical center is only open two hours a day for crew, and the 3 a.m.-4 a.m. time block was not one of them. So instead, we did what any well advised attendee at a college party would do—and no I don't mean take pictures and bribe her with them later, although I'm pissed that I am just now thinking of that—we slapped some poorly matched clothing on her and propped her up on her bed in the recovery position so she wouldn't choke on her own vomit. Because like Jimi Hendrix, I feel Elise still had a lot to offer the world.

Stories like this weren't exactly the exception to the rule when it comes to Elise's personal life. Throughout her first contract, she proved that she liked boys as well as girls, often at the same time. And she didn't discriminate. She would sleep with her boss, her coworkers, anybody in the entertainment department of all different nationalities. She was like the sexual ambassador of the United Nations, "making love not war" and spreading peace one night and multiple people at a time. I would like to take this time to thank Elise for only having relations once while I was in the bunk below, her track record far outshining my roommate during my freshman year of college.

While Elise seemed built for the cruise life, her flagrant disregard for the rules led us to create a chart of Vegas odds that she or I would be likely to commit. The lists consisted of things such as:

|           **Deedee**           |           **Elise**           |
| ------------------------------ | ----------------------------- |

1.  First to have their guitar completely destroyed:
        10/1                          3/1

Unfortunately I was the clear favorite for said event, as my guitar was the closest to the door and people busting in would subsequently slam into it, effectively knocking it on to whatever empty bottle lay on the floor below.

2. First to receive a written warning:
        3/1                          11/1

Elise took the odds here for a few reasons. She'd been on the ship for a shorter period of time and therefore had not been as familiar with the ridiculous rules as myself. Also, she was constantly drunk.

3. First to receive a verbal warning:
        4/1                          2/1

I had received a verbal warning for showing up a tad bit late to my 8 am shift one morning. Staying up until 5 am drinking in the orchestra pit with some new friends the night prior, combined with a room completely devoid of light, led to my sleeping through my alarm and two phone calls from my coworker. While my friend Riley said I should've acted like I read the schedule wrong and claimed ignorance, I had taken full responsibility for my tardiness. Granted, it was the only time in approximately 270 shifts that I was ever late, yet Pablo refused to let me live it down. I should've listened to Riley.

4. First to get cirrhosis of the liver:
     5/1                   9/1

These odds were based on science really. My liver had been training intensively for this contract for over six years in college, while Elise, although an admirable contender, was only exposed to sporadic nights of binge drinking induced regrets. Just like going 0-60mph too fast is bad for your car's transmission, so too is a rapid increase in alcohol consumption without proper training to your liver. Note: these odds were kept so close in the off chance that my scientific theory was not 100% accurate.

5. First to receive a negative comment card from a guest:
     2/1                   3/2

Only because Elise dealt with more people on a daily basis. Her odds were also hurt because of the VFW meetings she was sometimes require to host. Usually held early in the morning, Elise was almost always in a state of disarray and she noticeably upset at least one Veteran when she neglected to thank them for their sacrifice. A significant misstep given the heavily Texan population. The fact that she was Australian didn't get her out of thanking our American heroes for protecting our land.

6.  First to get fired:
         10/1                           7/1

Yes, I realize that our odds of developing serious liver-related diseases were greater than our odds of getting fired, but these statistics were put together with the lack of adequate security and ample amounts of readily available alcohol in mind. Elise took the edge here solely because she was still within her 90 day probationary period, meaning the company could fire you for any reason under the sun, and then a few more. I wasn't quite sure what set this "probationary period" apart from the at-will employment that we were all subject to. Under both premises you could be fired for good cause, bad cause, or no cause at all and RCI would suffer no repercussions (assuming the termination was not in violation of a statute protecting, well, protected traits, such as race, country of origin, or sex).

God only knows if any of this mattered to a U.S. company, staffed with foreign workers, built in Finland, registered to the Bahamas, and captained by a Norwegian, but I decided to give myself the benefit of the doubt and assume I would outlast Elise in any termination scenario. Boy had I miscalculated.

# CHAPTER XII: THE BEGINNING
# OF THE END

*Lesson I've learned the hard way #171: Never pass up an opportunity to TP the promenade.*

The beginning of the end actually began on land, right before I was flown out to Rome to embark on the aforementioned adventure. Remember that incredibly important reason I could not join the ship on the day Javier had originally requested? My college homecoming weekend that I already had flights for? Well you see, my friend Jonathon Brouse had actually paid for the tickets, so I would have felt doubly bad letting them go to waste. As you know, I was able to reschedule my join date to make it back to Oxford, Ohio for the weekend, and while I was at a social gathering of old college chums, I ran into my friend Kerry Brady.

"So what are you up to these days, Deeds?" Kerry asked.

"Actually, in a few days I'm gonna be working on a cruise ship as part of the sports staff for Royal Caribbean."

"That sounds amazing! A bunch of friends and I are actually going on a Royal Caribbean cruise for spring break. What ship are you on?"

"*Voyager of the Seas.*"

"No way, I think that's the one we're taking!"

And the conversation went on like this for another fifteen minutes or so, heavily influenced by the Nati Lite that was overflowing the cups.

We exchanged contact information so we could meet up during her spring break. None of us could have predicted then, that this conversation would eventually lead to such a catastrophe.

Fast forward to March 7, 2010, when Kerry and seven of her friends boarded the *Voyager of the Seas.* Let me try to explain what has to happen if you wish to be granted permission to socialize with your friends on a Royal Caribbean ship whilst a crewmember. After asking several different people, and receiving several different answers, I generally came to consensus that as this was my first contract, I didn't qualify for the 10% discount if my family were to book a cruise through me. In fact, the only benefit I was able to pass on to my parents when they had come on a cruise to visit me earlier in the year was two reusable Coke cups, which scored them free soda for the week. Of course nobody gave these to me, I picked them up after guests had left them in the skate shop—a fact that I neglected to mention to my parents until right now. I'm sure my mom wouldn't mind drinking out of somebody else's garbage cup but my dad has standards. I was also able to finagle a free tour for them ATV-ing through the Mayan ruins, but this was because of my personal relationship with the tour office, and by that, I mean I was their on and off slave for months so they decided to throw me a bone.

Suffice it to say that for a new hire, RCI grants absolutely zero benefits to friends or family in your contract. I *believe*, and I say believe because nothing is clear on these damn ships, that if I had my own cabin, like an activities director or the head light technician, I could sign one person into my crew cabin for $10 a day after I had completed at least one contract. And the icing on the cake was that they weren't relegated to eating in the mess hall like the rest of us schlubs—they could actually eat with their guest! Not too shabby right? Unfortunately, it was clear that I would not be working on the cruise lines long enough to ever qualify for my own room. As mentioned earlier, I was looking at this experience as a way to see the world, meet new friends, maybe one day use as inspiration to write a best selling book, but I certainly don't think I could've made it my career. But this will be important to keep in mind for later.

Back to the "ability to socialize with friends onboard" process. I had to get a request form from the Cruise Director's office weeks in advance and fill out my friend's name and information.

"Where are you going with that?" asked the cruise director when I walked toward the exit with the form.

"Umm…I was going to fill it out?"

"You can't do it now?" he asked, noticeably agitated.

"Well…no. It asks for her passport number." Who did he think I was Rain Man?

"Alright, just stick it outside my door when you're done."

"Will do."

As I slowly backpedaled out of his office, I also noticed that your request required approval. This form was not just letting them know that your friend was coming on a cruise and you want to see them, it had to be approved and signed by two higher-ups. Suddenly I felt like I was in one of those teen dramas of the 90s where I've ventured down a bad path and my father has decided to more closely select whom I was allowed to be friends with. Like I was Steph Tanner and Kerry was the rebellious, sexually promiscuous smoker Gia Mahan from *Full House*. I'm not quite sure what they base their approvals on, but I did wonder if crew were actually denied the chance to fraternize with their visiting friends. And so I held my breath.

And held it, and held it, and then held it a little longer. As it turns out, nobody actually lets you know if you've been approved to eat at the dining room with your friends while they're here. As the countdown to Kerry's arrival got closer and closer, I asked the CPA (remember, the woman who gives you your paychecks that you don't want to piss off?) if I was all set with regard to socializing with my friends.

"Oh yea, probably, I would assume so. If you haven't heard that you've been denied I would just go to the dining room with them. The Maitre D will kick you out if it wasn't approved."

Fantastic. As if I hadn't suffered enough public humiliation working here, let's throw in getting kicked out of the dining room in front of hundreds of people to the list. I suppose I could add, "first to get bitched out by the Maitre D" to our Vegas odds chart at least. So I rolled the dice.

When Kerry and her friends arrived, I met them outside the dining room and immediately felt a dozen crewmembers' eyes on me. I felt like I was harboring a Jew in Nazi Germany and I would be taken away at any second for breaking the law. But then again, I was the one wearing the metallic Star of David nametag as I entered the dining room. There was a lot of identity confusion that first night. My nerves were slightly calmed when I made it past the first line of defense in the dining room after explaining the situation to the host.

"Umm, you see...er...I know them...I got that paper thing signed saying I can eat with them? I...uh...I think it was approved, but nobody really told me...umm, I'll just head to the mess."

And as I bowed my head in disgrace and turned to walk away, I heard the host sing the beautiful words, "No ma'am that won't be necessary. Follow me."

It won't? Ma'am? It felt nice to be treated with some respect around here—must've been my overwhelming confidence and smooth talking that got me in. Just when I was starting to feel as if I didn't have that red dot between my eyes with a sniper behind it ready to pull the trigger, it hit me. Actually, it hit everybody in the dining room. The glare that was reflecting off of my metallic nametag on to what seemed like every piece of china, silverware, and chandelier in the three-story dining room. Ironman's fluorescent chest drew fewer stares. I made a note to wear a sweater the next night.

Our Filipino waiter came over to take our orders and was, of course, immediately drawn to the shiny object on my dress like a moth to a flame. There was less resentment than I had expected to feel from a fellow coworker who was now being told he had to serve me. *Much* less than when we won crew BINGO. I'm sure the fact that I was a white westerner didn't win me any favors with the wait staff. I had never seen a member of the crew (laundry, dining room, bartenders, etc. I know it gets confusing when I use the term "crew" to signify all workers but technically I was staff, so try to bare with me), ever get a chance to eat in the dining room. What happens if their families come onboard? Do they have to eat in the mess still? Are their families allowed to come onboard? After devoting twenty years of service to Royal Caribbean do they qualify for the same benefits as somebody like myself would in two? The answer was a clear no, and yet they all still seemed so happy.

Working 80-100 hours a week doesn't exactly give you a chance to get off the boat much, and doing it for nine months without a single day off seems like it would crush any soul I know. How terrible must the situation in their homelands be to come back year after year for $50 a month? But then again, you do get a really cool 5-year pin. It also reminded me that no matter how much I complained about my job and second-class citizenship on the *Voyager*, it could always get worse. And so I enjoyed my steak and after dinner drinks at the passenger-only Pig & Whistle Pub, preparing myself for when reality would set back in. I assumed however, that I would have a little more than 24 hours to do so. I was wrong.

# CHAPTER XIII: MOMENTS OF GOLD & FLASHES OF LIGHT

*Lesson I've learned the hard way #175:*
*Sometimes nights of endless pleasure are*
*actually more than any laws allow.*

The next morning in Honduras there was an all crew boat drill, in which, after reporting to our muster stations and waiting for forty minutes, we were given the unfortunate order to actually load the lifeboats. Most of you I'm sure have not experienced the misery of actually sitting in a lifeboat—unless your ship went down, in which case it was probably an awesome place to be. Picture a blistering hot sun, couple it with what seems like 300% humidity, add a heat retaining life vest around your neck, cram 150 people into a nauseatingly rocky boat the size of a closet, and you might have an idea of what it's like to be in a lifeboat in Honduras. With the layered seating, people are literally sitting on top of each other, ass to elbows (literally if you're part of the 75% unfortunate enough to get seats in the middle rows).

While we were incredibly thankful that we did not have to board the lifeboats *before* they were lowered into the water, it makes you wonder what the hell good it is preparing for a scenario that would never happen. I can't imagine a situation a docked ship would lower its lifeboats, have all the people debark a ship onto land, and then get right back into lifeboats. Maybe if a herd of bulls comes charging at people debarking the ship and the lifeboats happen to be down? Even so, I can't imagine that situation resulting in people slowly and orderly walking onto a lifeboat as we were. Maybe they were trying to see if the boats could still support the weight of 150 people, although I'm not sure how much buoyancy boats lose over a lifetime, but I can tell you that if it did start to sink about 85% of us would have perished with it due to enclosure of the boats.

I should note that I just sat at my desk for a solid fifteen minutes trying to conjure up a circumstance in which this drill would mimic a real life situation and that was the best I could come up with. If I had just joined the ship I would have assumed that they knew what they were doing and that there *had* to be a legitimate reason for it, but after spending any amount of time working for Royal Caribbean I realized that this was typically not the case. Regardless, we had all learned the futility of questioning any of these methods long ago, thus a 90-minute boat drill prevented me from meeting up with my friends in Honduras.

This had been the third night that my friends were onboard and I had mentioned to Jason that we were planning to go to the Vault that night for Kerry's birthday. Jason then took it upon himself to mention it to everybody else. He had of course asked me the degree of the girls' attractiveness, and once I confirmed that none of them were missing any limbs (not that that would've stopped him), he jumped at the idea of throwing an unofficial staff party. The Vault, as mentioned earlier, is the passenger discothèque that we, as privileged members of the staff, are allowed to patron. Though, along with everything else, there were rules. We had to be wearing the attire for the night—smart casual—with nametags, we were only allowed on the second floor of the Vault, and if we wanted to go to the first floor to dance, and *only* to dance, that was permitted. But so help you God if you didn't go straight upstairs after leaving the dance floor.

At around 9:30 that evening, eight of my coworkers and I made our way to the club after pre-gaming in our cabin for half an hour. Our salaries didn't last quite as long in passenger bars as they did at the back deck; so pre-gaming was always necessary prior to a Vault trip. However, knowing the bartenders has its benefits, and four shots per cocktail was the understood minimum for employees. Random free drinks and serving employees who were under 21 was not unheard of either. Of course we had to charge *those* drinks to *our* crew cards, as the Unders' cards were a phosphorescent yellow, making them just a tad more conspicuous.

To be honest, I didn't quite understand the rationale behind prohibiting 18 year-olds from drinking while we were in the Caribbean. For one, the idea that an 18-year-old seaman would not be able to drink is laughable, but there is also the whole "Flags of Convenience" thing. Remember the fact that they have to follow the laws of the country that the ship was registered to? Bahamian law—still sounds like a bit of an oxymoron to me—states that one can drink at 18, but in my experience anybody who can reach the counter gets served. Even when we were in the Mediterranean the drinking age was 18. So why, I ask you America, do you feel the need to regulate the drinking age on ships that serve U.S. ports, and not, say, working conditions? Or pay? Was this the compromise you made with cruise ships docking in your ports?

"Okay, okay, you guys can sail out of Miami if you promise not to let any of our citizens get murdered."

"No."

"Alright, ummm, how about if you try a bit harder to make sure there are no bed bugs in the passengers sheets?"

"No."

"Allow workers to unionize?"

"No."

"Hire credible doctors?"

"No."

"Perform a rape kit when there are allegations of sexual assault?"

"No."

"Pay taxes to the U.S. government like other U.S. companies?"

"Fuck no."

"Promise to cooperate with the FBI if there is foul play on a ship?"

"No."

"Pay overtime for working over 40 hours a week?"

"No."

"Make the drinking age 21?"

"Sure."

"Yessssssss."

Nicely done fellas. Just a little something to make working on a ship for months at a time just a little less tolerable for those under 21.

As I was saying, we were drunk. As more friends continued to shuffle in after their work duties had finished, the rowdier the third floor of the Vault became. There were spa girls, cruise staff, youth staff, sports staff, production staff, singers, dancers, musicians, and skaters. Hell, even the Loyalty & Cruise Sales guy was there and he was classy. It was one of those nights that you rely on pictures to piece together what happened when your memory goes blank. And go blank it did, but not for another hour or so. I distinctly remember shots of tequila lining the bar on multiple occasions for some thirsty crewmembers. There was a beautifully stacked pyramid of two-dozen glowing cups on display at the bar that came crashing to the ground when one of the spa girls pummeled into it. Crew was unsuccessfully attempting to break dance without spilling their drinks all over the floor. I wouldn't be surprised if somebody had been swinging from the chandelier. And then Kerry and her friends showed up.

That's right, all of this boisterousness had taken place before 11 p.m., which wouldn't bode well for how the rest of the night would go. After introducing Kerry and her friends to some of my friends who I best judged could form coherent sentences, more drinks were shoveled out when they realized it was her birthday. I guess in some cultures it's rude to make the birthday girl do shots by herself, a phenomenon I had not encountered in my personal experience.

We had typical alcohol-influenced banter, probably more talk about jumping overboard, who everybody's ship crush was, and at some point, I showed Kerry how our magnetic nametags worked. A concept that I realize now is less than fascinating. But at the time it drew the attention of a few more people, my roommate included. She decided she wanted to be me for the night because of that fancy Spanish flag I had so cunningly acquired. Elise and I switched nametags, and I was showing Kerry that I understood how some of the basic properties of magnetism work by affixing Elise's nametag to her shirt. Nobody thought much of it at the time—nobody thought much of anything at the time—but who can predict when the trivial will become tragic? Turns out, that thoughtless action would come back to bite a few of us in the ass.

As the night went on good times were had by all, with the possible exception of the security guards. They had witnessed the entire night of debauchery take place knowing full well that about 50% of the entertainment staff would be fired if breathalyzed at the moment. While I still maintain that they appreciated our interpretive dancing to Celine Dion's *It's All Coming Back to Me Now*, I'm sure the fraternizing with guests, knocking over displays, and body shots were held in lower esteem. This is when the details get hazy—that is to say hazier. The bar on the third floor (the only one the staff could go to in the Vault) closed what we all suspected was early, though nobody could say for sure what time. We assumed security had requested it close in order to get us out of the public view and into the crew bar where our drinking wouldn't be so, well, public. Because as Chapter 10 showed us: Alcohol + Seamen = Sex. And Sex (Seamen + Guest) = Termination with possibility of lawsuit.

Kerry's friends had decided to turn in; the Honduran sun had not been so kind to them that day and they were ready to call it night. However, Kerry had consumed just enough to not know when to say "enough," and decided to come with me to the crew bar. Though we all took different paths, all of the crewmembers managed to congeal at our favorite watering hole in the back of the ship. Leaving the Vault on Deck 3, we headed to the back of the ship, through the ice arena, up the photo gallery to Deck 4, outside the ship and then down the steps again to the crew bar. And don't blame the route on the booze; that was actually the most efficient way to get there. Nay, I should say, "that was the most efficient way to get there while retaining even the slightest bit of common sense." A concept that was lost on Katie, the 18 year old American dancer whose neglect of, and general disdain for sense of the common persuasion would lead to everybody's demise.

I'm not sure if it was the ego of a dancer, the hormones of a teenage girl or the alcohol running through her 18 year old veins, but Katie decided that the best thing she could do when the Vault had closed to crew was to invite four random male guests to the crew bar. Not such an unforgiveable move to the point where I would insult the integrity of a dancer—some of my other friends and I had snuck guests into the crew before. Where Katie went horribly wrong, however, was when she chose to take the absolute shortest path to the back deck. Unfortunately, this just so happened to be through the entire I-95, an all crew floor that spanned the length of the 1000+ foot ship and took them right past the security office. And just in case there weren't any auditory clues of five intoxicated people walking past security, Katie happened to be flashing one of those fashionable neon yellow crew cards on her belt…you know, the kind that identifies her as one of those members of society we don't allow to indulge in libations? Apparently security thought this was *too* big of an insult to let slide and followed the group to the crew bar.

Meanwhile, Kerry and I had been in the crew bar for a few minutes when security came in and, as they rounded up the random passengers, asked her to "please come with them." Now, before I launch into my heroic tale of going after her, let me just explain how I had literally seen dozens of crewmembers bring their families and friends to the back deck, including our noble leader Mark, the cruise director. Not once has anybody ever said anything to them, nor had I seen anybody even nervous about bringing them there.

This, combined with the fact that friends and family could be signed into a crewmember's actual crew cabin led me to believe that friends were permitted in certain crew areas under certain circumstances. Had this not been the case, I probably would have told Kerry to pretend she didn't know me and that she had gotten lost trying to find her way back to her cabin. But no, assuming there was no wrongdoing on my part, I went to clear things up. As I followed Kerry and security into the slop chest room right outside the bar, I saw the four random strangers that Katie had brought up getting written up by other security "officials."

"Wait you guys made a mistake. She's my friend, I signed her on before she boarded."

"What is your name and cabin number?" the large Indian security guard asked.

"Deedee Presser, 4271...but I don't understand, I signed her in," I said confused both by their ambiguous rules and the large amount of alcohol in my system at the moment.

"You signed her in?"

"Yes, my slip should be in the security office."

"Okay, go back to your room."

"Yes, sir. Bye, Kerry," I whispered to my friend and sprinted out of there.

Jason informed me that while this was taking place outside in the slop chest, inside the bar an actual fistfight had broken out between him and Riley over Katie and everybody who had gotten caught in the middle of it joined in. Chairs were tossed, drinks were spilled and even black eyes were received by a few. But security was doing their best to make this a safe ship by "writing people up," whatever that even meant.

Turns out it meant quite a bit, but I'll get to that later. As I made it back to my room, I was talking to some of the dancers who were in our hallway when I heard the news. Katie had apparently bolted with Jackson (the other 18 year old dancer) when security picked up the four random men she had brought to the crew bar. But whatever she had consumed that night was affecting her teenage body too strongly to go unnoticed the *second* time she staggered by the security office on the I-95.

In an unprecedented event, security saw her neon yellow crew card and put two and two together. They breathalyzed her as well as Jackson, who also had the unfortunate luck of being screwed over by Katie that night. Blowing a blood alcohol level of .08 or higher meant you were legally drunk according to ship law, and being "drunk" as a crewmember on a ship was never technically allowed as mentioned earlier. Granted, in Ireland a .08 is a necessity to getting through a workday, and on a ship it's a requisite to living. And while Royal Caribbean doesn't see fit to follow any U.S. labor or tax laws, for some reason they chose to adopt their legal limit of alcohol.

Being breathalyzed was serious though. It was right on par with hitting or sleeping with a guest. While both were fun, there's a 99% chance of getting fired if found guilty. And although Katie and Jackson were slightly more important since they knew the dance routines, their moves probably wouldn't be enough to save them. I can't remember exactly what the dancers blood alcohol levels were that evening (knowledge that I have somehow managed to live without for years), I do remember it being well over the legal limit.

So, the night had ended on a more somber note than it had started, but nothing could be changed at this point and everybody went to bed. Well, most people went to bed...some people had sex on the bunk bed above me that night, but that was strangely less odd than seeing the ship security crack down on the crew that night, and I slept like a baby.

## CHAPTER XIV: THE AFTERMATH

*Lesson I've learned the hard way #180: In the event that you will have to meet with the Chief of Security, wake up ten minutes earlier to take a shower.*

What's even more impressive than sleeping through intercourse in the bunk above mine was that at some point in the night, my mind had the foresight to set an alarm for my 8 a.m. shift of work the next day. I jumped out of bed, changed, threw some water on my face, brushed my teeth and went to grab a bagel in the mess before heading up to the jogging track to wait for the long-awaited first guest of my contract to show up for the "Walk-a-Mile." No dice.

After I realized that hour of my life was not coming back, I made my way to the Cruise Director's office to get ready for the boat drill. I was greeted, nay, reproached by Pablo, who had just returned two days earlier from his vacation. As if the prior night's festivities weren't bad enough, there was Pablo to compound my feelings of guilt.

"I was sent to get you," he said in his straight-faced-I-don't-know-if-I'm-about-to-get-reprimanded-or-promoted tone. Although given the context of last night's debauchery, I thought it was safe to assume it was the former.

"Oh...okay, where are we going?" I asked, hoping he was about to give me a free tour of Honduras.

"Chief of Security has summoned for you."

While I didn't like the sound of that, the word "summoned" *did* make me feel like a classy type of criminal, the kind who goes to a tribunal while all of the other yokels go to a regular court.

"But I'm gonna miss boat drill," I replied, as if it were all of a sudden my favorite thing to do while on an exotic island.

"This is okay, it has been approved."

Oh shit. This was now a matter of urgency? Matters of urgency with the Chief of Security, unless identifying a murder suspect or describing when a passenger was last seen before falling off the boat, were never good. And I hadn't seen any murders or man over-boards last night, so I'm guessing this had to do with my friend coming to the crew bar. I told Pablo what had happened and he offered about as much solace as I had expected him to, which is to say none. Instead of telling me that it would be a warning at most like my friends had, he launched into stories about people he knew who had been fired for lesser offenses, made to walk the plank, and then tarred and feathered if they made it to dry land.

As we made it to the British bloke's office, I thought Pablo was about to bow on his knees to the man as I watched his already brown nose get even browner.

"Hello sir, I brought her down as you asked. I would also like to say that this is only the third day I've been back from my vacation."

After looking at Pablo as if he wasn't quite sure who he was, Mike asked me where I was in the morning when he phoned my room.

"I was at work," I replied, still half disgusted with Pablo's groveling and extra happy that I had set my alarm.

"She didn't have to work until 8 a.m. sir," Pablo chimed in, offering any information that might get him a "thanks," or a "job well done," from Mike. What an incredible kiss-ass.

"I called three minutes to 8 so that makes sense," he said, wiping the look of hope from Pablo's face. Then he turned to me. "So tell me what happened last night."

Well if that wasn't an open-ended question... I decided to start from the beginning.

"I had signed my friend Kerry Brady in before she came onboard for her vacation. I've been dining with her for the past couple of nights, and last night was her birthday. When the Vault closed I took her to the crew bar. We were in there for about five minutes and security came in and escorted her out, and I went to clear things up." I decided to give him the abridged version.

He checked his files, found all the paperwork that had been processed in order for me to converse with my friend on the ship and looked it over. "Why was your friend wearing Elise Garrison's name badge?"

Blast! That damn name badge had come back to haunt us. Instead of telling him the truth, which involved us being blackout drunk and finding anything amusing at the time, including swapping identities for the night, I felt it was necessary to take a different route. "Elise is my roommate and I had mistakenly taken her nametag that night. I was just showing Kerry how the magnetic name badge worked and never took it back off of her." It was interesting to note that the part of this story that made sense was the lie and the part that didn't make sense to the sober mind was actually true.

"I need you to fill out an incident report."

Shit.

As I began filling out the incident report, I couldn't help but feel like this was quite an over-reaction to the event that had actually taken place, much like that time a friend and I were pulled over by *two* police cars for saran wrapping our other friend's car. Small towns are similar like that I guess.

"Umm...Mike? This says, "perpetrator" and "victim" at the top, what do I fill out for that?"

"That's you, you're the perp."

Wow. A week ago this man was showing me card tricks at the dinner table and now he was calling me a perp. I guess loyalty on the high seas has remained remarkably consistent throughout time, a fact that several early explorers learned the hard way.

I wrote down the details that I had told Mike, about my roommate Elise not having anything to do with the entire situation, about how I was under the impression that if you signed your friend in you had the green light to take them to the crew bar (for the simple reasons that I had seen several of my superiors do the same and they were allowed in crew areas if you signed them into your cabin), etc. When I handed it to Mike he remarked, "You smell of alcohol," in an accent reminiscent of that bloody GEICO gecko.

Now my sense of smell has always been my weakest sense. I can identify a skunk and gasoline, but that's about it. I was once at a science museum with ten of the most common scents that were hidden in boxes and had to be identified by the nose; I went a less-than-perfect 0 for 10. The old olfactory sense, or lack there of, really hurt me today though. Caught totally off guard I replied, "Really? It should smell like cream cheese." Not the most well thought out response I admit, but what the hell are you supposed to say when a giant security guard looks you in the eye and tells you that you smell like alcohol at nine in the morning? I panicked.

As I walked out of the security office, my friend Cara was walking in after being written up for something that happened last night as well. The security office looked like the DMV that morning. Elise and a few others were summoned in also. This was apparently the trial of the freakin' century and security was sparing no expense when it came to interviewing "witnesses."

After trying to corroborate stories with other crewmembers and figure out what exactly happened last night, I spent the rest of the day replaying the past 24 hours in my head. If I had woken up 15 minutes earlier to take a shower would that have helped my cause? Can you even shower off alcohol? Should I not have gone after Kerry when security dragged her out? After all, nothing happened to the guests found in the crew bar. Clearly I shouldn't have put the nametag on her, but of all the things that happened that night, who would've guessed that *that* would have been the most incriminating action? If putting a nametag on a friend turns out to be the stupidest thing I do when I'm drunk then I will consider myself lucky. And then I dissected the security meeting. Why didn't he give me a written warning? Was that a good or a bad thing? Given the nature of the offense I didn't think it would be unheard of to walk away with a slap on the wrist, but given the nature of ships I knew that most of what they did didn't make much sense.

"Well, I got to miss boat drill at least..." was the only thing I could conclude decisively after the meeting and I set off to meet my friends on the island of Roatán, Honduras. I said my goodbyes to George, the curious and affectionate monkey that was a staple of the island, "just in case." After a beautiful day of snorkeling and lounging with friends I returned to the ship and saw Adam, a sound technician who was constantly asking people if they wanted to TP the promenade with him.

"Hey so I heard you had a meeting with Mike today? Any new inclination to TP the promenade?"

"Hah, Adam you know I've always wanted to do that, but we both know I'm too big of a coward."

"Let me know if you change your mind."

I would live to regret this, although considering the fact that there could've been jail time or fines, I suppose it was for the best that I did not. I also had the unfortunate luck to run into the security chief again.

"Hey, I need you to meet me at 2 p.m. tomorrow in my office."[41]

"Okay." I responded and cowered away without further questioning because I am spineless. What the hell does he want to see me again for? Were they going to kick me off the boat in Costa Maya? Is that legal? I'm sure it is by their rulebook. Should I go TP the ship with Adam real quick? Questions were once again racing through my mind.

I ate dinner with Kerry and her friends again that night and they were all curious as to what had transpired at the meeting with security. I disclosed the information quietly, because you never know who's listening on a ship, and Kerry chimed in. I believe her exact words were, "I've always considered myself to have psychic abilities and I have a good feeling about this, don't worry." Or something to that effect. She then mentioned that she had brought tarot cards on the ship with her.

I did not have a whole lot of confidence in the entire realm of supernatural processes, a healthy skepticism I have due in part to a terribly inaccurate palm reading in New Orleans. Nevertheless, it would make for a more interesting

---

[41] After leaving my friends on shore early again to receive another lashing by Mike, he never showed up. I was glad that I didn't have to sit through another lecture on the dangers of passengers in crew areas, but I was oddly angry that he didn't deem my "crime" worthy enough to show up to his own meeting.

lunch so I obliged. On Friday, two days before the end of the cruise, Kerry brought her devil cards to the Windjammer buffet and gave me a reading.

"Okay so cut and shuffle the deck for me please."

I shuffled and cut the deck.

"The first three cards I flip over will represent your current situation, and the last three cards I flip over are your future."

I slowly nodded my head at Kerry trying to decide if she belonged in a straight jacket or on Oprah. The first three cards were eerily accurate.

They involved feelings of anxiousness and stress, a big decision about to be made by higher authority figures, and illustrated that all of this was weighing on my mind. Check. The next three went as follows:

Card #1: I can't remember.

Card #2: I will never forget. It showed a picture of a woman sitting on a bed by herself with her head in her hands crying. Just to add to the already ominous card, there were spear-like objects cutting through the top of the card above the woman. Now I've never taken a class in tarot reading, but this did not look promising. I was hoping in the tarot world things weren't what they seemed. Like, maybe this girl had a problem and the spears were there to eradicate it? But as luck would have it, this was not the case. I guess that picture is universal in its meaning and would later be validated.

Card #3: This card seemed to seal my fate. It depicted a person who was waving goodbye to something and there was an ocean in the background coupled with a setting sun. Kerry explained that this was me saying goodbye to something and starting something new. "Well that's good, I think it probably means that you're saying goodbye to land as you set off on another cruise," she explained.

"Couldn't it mean that I'm waving goodbye to all of my friends and my life on the ship as I stay on land?"

"Well…yes. I suppose. But I'm choosing to take it the other way."

I think she just noticed how disappointed I was that she had made no attempt to spin that crying lady card positively a minute earlier. Well that certainly didn't give me any confidence about my current situation. It did, however, lend credence to Kerry's psychic abilities. So there's that.

After lunch, I continued to run through my normal workday of belaying and leading ping-pong tournaments, when three guests excitedly came up to me.

"Oh my God the other night was crazy, huh?!" the tall one said in reference to the infamous Tuesday. Of course I had no idea who they were or what they were talking about at the time.

After I gave some uncomfortable laughter and silence as I frantically tried to think of how I knew them and what they were talking about, I segued into the heart of the conversation. "What?" I asked them.

- 227 -

"Oh man, you don't remember us, do you? Did you get into trouble on Tuesday? We're so sorry if you did."

And then it hit me. They were three of the four random guys that Katie had dragged up to the crew bar, passing by security on the I-95. I don't ever recall actually talking to any of them, but maybe they saw me trying to defend myself to security as they were being "disciplined" by other officials in the slop chest room.

"Oh yeah, um, thanks. Well I'm actually probably going to be fired, so if you could write me some good reviews on your comment cards maybe they'll at least feel bad about it."

"No shit really!? That seems a little harsh. We'll for sure write you good reviews. Any chance you'll be out tonight?"

"Yeah, but I probably shouldn't hang out with guests that I didn't sign on. Figure that probably won't help my case, should my fate not be sealed quite yet."

"Ah yeah, good idea. Yeah they didn't do anything to us. I thought we might get kicked off or fined or something, but nope. They just told us not to do it again and sent us on our merry way."

"Congratulations," I said with what might have possibly been construed as a hint of sarcasm.

"Welp, see ya later!" they said as they walked away.

"Maybe on the plane," I shot back, hoping that wouldn't be the case.

That Saturday night, the last night of the cruise, we all went through the ordeal that was *Waves*, where all the staff members smile and wave goodbye with cheesy music to the passengers one last time. Afterward, I went to the dining room to eat quickly with Kerry and her friends before hurrying off to the Windjammer. Traditionally we had been going there after every *Waves*, and paying the $3 fee for crew (for guests it was free, sort of a reverse employee discount if you will) to change up the scenery and caliber of food every week. I hadn't planned on going this week since my friends were cruising, but I wanted to play it safe should this be the last time I ever see some of my ship friends. I figured I'd probably see Kerry in Ohio before I see any of my friends from the Ukraine, India or Indonesia. Not that those countries aren't at the top of my list—they aren't—but trying to coordinate a meet up with somebody who works on a cruise ship is like solving those Level 5 sudoku puzzles on the ship; difficult and often unsuccessful. At least if this was going to be my last meal, I'd be going out in style: a $3 buffet of whatever the ship had left over by the end of the weeklong cruise.

That night we headed from the Windjammer back to our rooms to change into our sweats (well, *I* changed into sweats) and then continued to the back deck to mark the end of another cruise with libations for all. I kept my night to a respectable four drinks—probably the least amount of alcohol consumed in the history of "end of cruise nights," for fear that security would be watching me. Everybody turned in at around 3:00 a.m. to try and salvage some sleep before our mornings would start all too soon. My roommate Elise's began at 6:15 a.m. with debark duty. I had a different kind of wake up when I received a phone call from Jack, the Activities Manager, saying that I had a Captain's Hearing at 8 a.m. and he would be at my room in 15 minutes to walk me there. When he hung up the phone. I responded sleepily, "What?"

Did I have Captain's Hearing duty this morning? I don't remember seeing that on my schedule. I don't even know what that is? Do passengers get to listen to the sounds of the Captain's room? What the hell is going on?

After about 3 minutes of trying to open my eyes to full capacity my grogginess wore off and I put it together. Oh. That was like a trial, only without the right to an attorney or a jury of your peers. Just five of the most powerful men on the ship sitting at the end of a long oval table facing you, the "perpetrator." Also, you are not given any time to prepare any type of a defense, or to wake up with the hope of stringing sentences together to formulate a coherent thought. And you are presumed guilty until proven innocent. It's how I imagine the Chinese justice system to be.

My memory is not so sharp with regard to what happened in the ensuing minutes, as I was slowly coming back to consciousness, but I believe I took what is possibly one of the quickest and least effective showers in my life. While in the shower, I gave my teeth a solid scrub down with a hearty amount of toothpaste, hoping to avoid the pitfalls of my last meeting with an authority figure, and making sure their was neither alcohol nor cream cheese on my breath. I threw on my uniform and triple checked that *my* nametag was affixed to the upper left quadrant of my shirt at a 90-degree angle to my collarbone per SQM standards (I'm sure it's probably in there somewhere). As soon as I thought about drying my hair there was a knock at the door.

It was Jack. Sweet Jack. The twenty-something year old, levelheaded boy from Tennessee. And now he was acting as a U.S. Marshall extraditing me to a new holding cell. This vision replaced the previously held picture I'd had of him in my mind of the man who had a threesome with my lesbian roommate and a British dancer his first week on the *Voyager*. How the times and circumstances had changed.

I can honestly say I was not that nervous as we trudged to the luxurious residence of the Captain. Probably because I still wasn't 100% awake, but also because I assumed I was just going up there to get a written warning. After all, what had been my crime? I brought a friend to a bar in a crew area. I had brought my parents to see my cabin when they were visiting without thinking twice. Hell, if I had my own room I could've signed them in to *stay* in a crew area.

Jack and I waited outside the Captain's room for 10 minutes; I guess the Jamaican bartender they were in the process of firing was not taking it very well. After an enormous amount of shouting and several pleas of, "but how will my family eat now!?", it was my turn. My nervousness took a considerable jump.

A very small percentage of people in this world have had the experience of working on a cruise ship, and those who have been on the wrong side of a Captain's Hearing comprise an even smaller percentage. It is my hope that this is as close to one as any of you will ever get. I've thrown myself out of a plane, as well as off a bridge, and came dangerously close to the Gaza Strip, but this was worse. Not in the way that I thought a landmine might blow my legs off, but in the way a refugee is deported back to their war torn country after months of living in peace. Okay, I guess that's also a poor analogy. Let's just say, it sucks.

And I realize now that the book up until this point may have come off as one giant complaint: about the medical staff, the lack of respect, the poor working conditions, the low pay, the inefficiency of being paid, the food, the nametags in the gym, the fact that I can't drink tea in front of guests, etc. But the truth is, I adapted to it, and I learned to love it. It was like a drug addiction. I knew deep down that it was probably not the best for me, but it could be such a high that I would be devastated if I couldn't get a hit of that sweet cruise life.

As I entered the room, I couldn't help but notice just how massive the Captain's quarters were, compared to everybody else's on the ship of course, and was hoping my first time in them would not be my last day on the ship. Once the shock of how the other half lived wore off, I focused my attention on the intimidating scene that was laid out before me. Dressed in my royal blue warm-ups and arched eyebrows, I was facing a fifteen foot mahogany table surrounded by the five most powerful people on the ship in their fanciest uniforms and their furrowed eyebrows. Needless to say, I felt a little underdressed. Their name and ranks were as follows:

| | |
|---|---|
| Peter Rohl | Master |
| Trond Dahl | Staff Captain |
| Condolize Malrenu | Hotel Director |
| Daniel Burr | H.R. Manager |
| Mark Sarkowski | Cruise Director |

The hearing started off as any would, having me state my name and rank, which was weird seeing as there was no recording or stenographer there.

"My name is Deedee Presser. I am currently a member of the sport staff."

"When did you join the ship, Deedee?"

"I joined mid-cruise in Rome the last week of October." *After having a hell of a time finding my way to the ship after you bastards abandoned me at the airport in a foreign country whose language I did not speak.* Note, my filters were working at this time and I refrained from saying this last part.

"So you have been with the ship for approximately five months? Have you attended all of the trainings?"

"Yes."

"Have you noticed the yellow signs indicating that guests were not allowed in crew areas?"

"Yes, I've seen them. But as I stated in my incident report I was under the impression that the signs were referring to random guests that have not been signed in by the employee. Since we're allowed to sign guests into our rooms, which I believe also constitute "crew areas," I believed the categories of guests were different."

"Why was your friend wearing a name badge?"

Hmm...good question. Do I answer it truthfully and admit the appeal of shiny objects when I am half in the bag? Or do I come up with something less incriminating? Hurry up Deedee there are five sets of authoritative eyes on you waiting for five more seconds of silence to confirm your guilt. I think this is the type of question an attorney would've prepared me for, if I'd had access to counsel, so I wasn't sitting there thinking on my feet like an ass.

Flashbacks to an old internship interview rushed back into my mind. It was like when they had asked me five things to do with a pencil. Everybody knows "stab somebody with it" has to be one of the top five uses of a pencil, right? But who's going to say that in an interview? You wouldn't get the job at best; you'd be committed at worst. SPEAK! Deedee, for the love of God, speak!

"Umm...well, my friend had never seen a magnetic nametag before and I wanted to show her how much nicer they were than the pins. So I put it on her and then got distracted and forgot to take it off of her."

Now before you start judging, I know how juvenile it sounds, okay? I am also assuming if you've ever had two long island iced teas on top of tequila shots, anything looks impressive. Even magnetic nametags. I can, with 100% honesty, say that I was not trying to sneak Kerry past security using a company nametag. It's not like every employee on the ship doesn't recognize every other employee on the ship anyway. That'd be almost as dumb as not realizing Clark Kent is Superman because he has glasses and a suit on. And even in my most inebriated state I would be able to identify Superman.

"Uh-huh," Captain Peter said as he scribbled something down in his notes. Something along the lines of, "make sure to give her a middle seat on the plane home today."

"And do you understand the implications of bringing a guest into crew areas and the danger it posed to them?"

Are you fucking kidding me? The crew bar poses more danger to crewmembers than it does to any guest on a nightly basis. If anything, a slightly more sober guest will probably talk a crewmember out of jumping off the back of the ship into the frigid water. Or be there to cushion a crewmembers fall when they pass out from drinking too much. Maybe they should require *more* guests back there.

No Peter, just what kind of danger is posed to a guest in the crew bar? Is it more or less dangerous than having your appendicitis diagnosed as diabetes by the ship medical center? These are the questions I would've asked if I weren't such a coward. Instead I answered, "I do now," referring to the danger that sometimes people receive Captain's Hearings when they bring friends to the back deck and sometimes

- 235 -

nothing happens. Unfortunately, I think Peter took that as a concession from me that conditions in the crew areas were actually more hazardous to guests than crewmembers.

"Step outside now please, we need to discuss things further."

As I excused myself from the table I couldn't help but feel like that could've gone better. I mean I did have a point; there is definitely a difference between guests you knew before they came on the ship and random guests you met that week. What is the point of the entire sign in process, in which I needed to acquire their birthday, address, and passport information in order to be seen with her in public areas, if I constantly needed to defend myself? And what other place would make having a beer with my friend after work seem like a criminal activity, besides Saudi Arabia, or the U.S. during Prohibition?

I waited for what seemed like a lifetime, but in actuality was probably about five minutes, when my conversation with Jack was interrupted by an angry, "We're ready." I entered again, aware of all the instances in which a short deliberation implied a guilty verdict, but maybe they had all realized just how stupid this entire ordeal was—I certainly had.

"Ms. Presser, do you like your job?"

"I love it," I responded, which I hadn't realized until just then. Granted it was a love/hate relationship, but there was definitely love there.

"I wish you had taken it more seriously then."

I don't, I thought to myself. That's *why* I loved it. I was working on a friggin' cruise ship for Christ's sake, not in an ICU. I don't think it's in my blood to be serious, and certainly not for $3/hr in a job where one of my main duties was wearing an oversized Tiki head in the "Island Frenzy" parade. Although I suppose I did take it more seriously than Jason, who literally had a guest complain *in writing* that he was drunk while belaying at the rock wall. But hey, five minutes of socializing with a friend at the crew bar does seem to pose more of a threat to the safety of our guests.

Still, I can say I was surprised when the Captain, whose right hand man's name was Trond, told me that I was, "being dismissed for 'gross misconduct' as per SQM Policy 6.08.3a. Which means you are banned from ever working for this company, or its sister company Celebrity Cruises ever again."

I couldn't help but laugh. And not in my head, I mean out loud, in front of the "counsel." Gross misconduct? A lifetime ban? Doesn't that all seem a little harsh? And a completely inaccurate description of what had transpired? A business dictionary defines "gross misconduct" as:

*Indiscipline so serious (such as stealing, or work place violence) that justifies the instant dismissal of an employee, even on the first occurrence. Examples include illegal drug use at work, stealing, sexual harassment, and assault and battery.*[42]

---

[42] http://www.businessdictionary.com.

Royal Caribbean's SQM Policy defines it as: well actually, I have no idea how Royal Caribbean defines gross misconduct because once again, we were never actually given or shown a copy of SQM Policy. I can tell you my Captain's Hearing form describes my personal case of gross misconduct as, "Employee brought a guest into crew areas." I couldn't help but notice that my defense of "knowing her and signing her onto the ship" went unmentioned. My pleas of, "But I knew her!!!" apparently fell on deaf ears, but would continue to close the story of how I got fired from a cruise ship every time I had to explain it to one of my friends.

Those who think it doesn't make a difference, you have obviously never worked on a cruise ship. Reflecting back on the hearing that night, my biggest regret is that I didn't throw the Cruise Director under the bus with me. Yes that's correct, the only thing I wish I hadn't done was accept their decision so graciously. That Jamaican bartender before me left in a furious rage while calling every member in the hearing something hilariously insulting, and I'm not sure but it sounded like he flipped a chair. He knew what was up.

You know that saying, "You'll never regret the things you do, only the things you don't do?" These words could not be more accurate. I regret not asking Mark (the cruise director) at the hearing if he was going to say anything on my behalf, since I had personally seen him bring no less than a dozen various friends to the crew bar, or all those times he played beer pong with guests in the backstage of the ice rink. But I didn't. And I regret it. I blame my parents for instilling some sort of civility in me that subconsciously told me the "right" thing to do was to accept their decision and walk out gracefully.

For those of you who may find yourself in a similar situation in the future, if there is no way that your employer will be able to communicate with future employers, I would absolutely recommend setting those bridges ablaze when you walk out. Things I also regretted *not* doing before I left (but not quite as much, seeing as how some of them may very well have led to legal action):

- Flipped a chair
- Toilet-papered the Royal Promenade
- Jumped off the ship from the 4th deck
- Cleaned out the bar with my crew card before it was cutoff
- Acquired a copy of the SQM manual so I could have actually confirmed its existence
- Washed my clothes
-Figured out a clever way to make fun of the name "Trond."

One of these days I can only hope to be debarking a cruise and witness the brilliant display of toilet paper strung about the main promenade in an act of defiance from a disgruntled employee. Then I will know that this book has made a difference.[43]

---

[43] Disclaimer: The author of this book maintains no responsibility for, and expressly disclaims all liability for, damages of any kind arising out of use, reference to, or

assumed they would pass the message along to anybody interested whose number I didn't have. I then adjusted the Vegas Odds chart Elise and I had in our room to increase my odds of being fired first to 99%, still taking into consideration that Elise had been working since 6:30 a.m. and who knows what had transpired in that kind of time?

By my estimates it would take approximately 7.5 minutes for word to spread around the entire ship; and, much like a game of telephone that message would probably lose detail and become supplanted with all kinds of crazy new facts such as, "Did you hear they fired that American sports staff for jumping off the ship for fun?" Or, "I heard she was fired for sleeping with a guest entertainer in the Royal Promenade bathroom." Since almost any rumor would be a more dramatic ending to my ship debacle than what had actually transpired, I was cool to let those slide. There would be a new and exciting message spreading around by tomorrow night anyway.

Perhaps the most tragic part of this all was that I had a full bottle of Jack Daniel's in my room that would not travel well. Never one to let an entire bottle of alcohol go to waste, and simply giving it to my friends was a waste by my logic, I made everybody take a shot with me as my going away present. Even Angela, the American trombone player took a shot, and she was one of the most sober people on the ship. As they helped me pack, we realized the vacuum bag that had been so helpful in squeezing all of my clothes into my bag when I had left for the ship required the assistance of an actual vacuum. After twenty minutes of tracking down the one vacuum on the ship available to crew, I realized it did not have a detachable handle, which was necessary for sucking the air out. We all attempted to use the long, horizontal head of the vacuum to suck the air out of a one-inch hole that it was designed for, but to no avail. My friend did however, succeed in cutting the bag open with a shard of a beer bottle that was stuck in the vacuum.

"Whatever, it doesn't matter. It wasn't gonna work with this vacuum anyway," I reassured him.

No less than a minute after we heard, "Do you guys need a smaller vacuum?" One of the room stewards asked us after he heard what was transpiring. "I have one right here if you need it."

My friend and I exchanged looks of frustration. Well, mine was a look of frustration, his was more apologetic. "This day keeps getting better and better," I said to him.

"And it's only just begun," he responded. "Your plane could go down, you could get in an accident driving to the airport, your house could be burned down when you get there... You should probably rub my half-Irish penis for good luck today."

"You're a good friend Riley, but you're not half-Irish, and I don't know if my tetanus shot is up to date."

"Trust me there's no rust on it," he said with a smirk.

"Just herpes then?"

"So far," he said jokingly. At least I'm pretty sure it was a joke.

"Well don't worry slugger, STDs are like baseball cards around here, you'll get the one you want with a little persuasiveness and persistence. Hey that reminds me have you seen Diego?"

"STDs remind you of Diego?"

I laughed, but the truth was, leaving him was going to be pretty difficult. As mentioned earlier, he was one of the only guys on the ship that wasn't a huge pervert, openly at least. It was a match made in heaven. Actually it was made in the steerage of a ship, as all great romances are.

I can say that while leaving Diego so abruptly was difficult, it was made slightly easier by the fact that he was not in his room when I went to say goodbye. He was working either debark or in Adventure Ocean, or possibly getting supplies, his roommate Tim couldn't remember.

"I'll tell him you stopped by. We're all gonna miss ya mate," Tim said somberly as he hugged me goodbye.

"Thanks Tim, I'm gonna miss you guys too. Make sure this ship doesn't get too lame without me on it."

"I'll do my best."

As I walked back down the hall to my room, I saw Elise running around the corner. She was still working debark but had heard the results of the Captain's Hearing and came to say goodbye on her break. As soon as we made eye contact we both started crying. I said the only thing I could muster, "I changed the odds on our board." This of course led to louder crying and tighter embracing.

There's not much more I really care to say about my goodbyes. It was sad. It was unexpected, blah blah blah. The good news was that I was just fired from a ship, and was not just diagnosed with cancer.

Fast-forward to the bus ride taking us to the airport. It was full of people whose contracts were over including the ice cast crew, and my friend Riley, as well as people who were fired, like Katie, Jackson and myself. Since my bag had still been far too full to fit my dirty laundry, I decided to just carry my dirty laundry bag and try to conceal it under my coat when I went to check in. As it was, I was carrying my guitar, my 50-pound luggage, and my 30-pound backpack. Looking back on it now, I probably should've just paid the extra money to check another bag, but at the time $60 to ship dirty laundry home did not seem worth it.

On the hour drive from Galveston to Houston, I had called my brother and my sister to ask their advice.

"Hey so I was just fired from the ship and am being flown home today. Should I not tell mom and dad and try to freak them out by showing up in the window or something? What do you think?"

Both answered a resounding, "Yes," and I worked out a plan to have my friend Meghan pick me up from the airport that day. Everything was set. Until I tried to get my boarding pass. Royal Caribbean had given me the itinerary with my leaving papers. I was evidently booked on a Delta flight from Houston to Hartford via Cincinnati.

"I'm here to check in," I told the woman at the counter as I handed her my license and information.

"Huh."

"Is something wrong?"

"Hmm...well when I type in your name it appears that you're going to Orlando."

"My ticket says right there that I'm going to Hartford," I said pointing to the destination line of my itinerary.

"Yes I see that, hence the 'huh.'"

After 15 minutes of her looking confused at her computer, she informed me that the computer had somehow cancelled my previous flight and booked another one for Orlando.

"That's never happened before," she said. "Huh."

Given the day I was having, I'll admit I was a little short with her.

"Well my flight is boarding in 20 minutes do you think you could hurry up and rebook it?"

"Well...you see I would...but, huh. It looks as if this flight to Cincinnati is booked. And there are no other flights that are going to Hartford today."

"It's 1:00p.m. How are there no other flights that connect to other flights that go to Hartford today?"

"Well it is Spring Break for a lot of schools."

"Ma'am have you ever *been* to Hartford, Connecticut? You think the Mark Twain house is a big draw for college kids these days? Or maybe it's the miserable cold? Do you think spring breakers are really interested in checking out the insurance capital of the world on their one week off in the semester? Believe it or not Houston would be a better choice for a spring break destination."

"Sorry, they're all full."

"Huh. Well, what can I do now?"

"You have to call this number," she said pointing to the sheet I had just handed her. "This is the Royal Caribbean travel agent number."

I dragged my entourage of luggage to the corner, and sat up against a wall. With my guitar case on the ground in front of me, a fucking *sack* of clothes next to me, and a combination of bloodshot eyes and disheveled hair, I looked like a legitimate hobo. Did I mention I couldn't have looked more defeated? Hobos usually looked defeated as well.

"This is my new life," I thought to myself as I tried a third time to contact the travel agent. Finally somebody answered.

"Hello?"

"Hi, I was told to call you because a flight Royal Caribbean booked me on was cancelled by a computer?" I said hoping she knew what I meant. "My name is Deedee Presser."

"Huh," she muttered. Here we go again. "Yes that's really weird I've never seen that before. And it looks like all the flights out of Houston to Hartford are booked solid."

"Yes, I hear the convention center looks beautiful this time of year."

"What?"

"Nothing. What am I supposed to do now?"

"I can book you on one early tomorrow morning."

"Tomorrow morning? So I am going to have to sleep on the streets tonight?" This hobo thing was getting a little too real.

"What? No, I will book you at the hotel nearby."

"Really? For free? Because if it comes down to paying for a hotel or sleeping at the airport I am willing to sleep at the airport."

"No ma'am, that won't be necessary, we'll cover it."

"Great, because quite frankly the Delta departure area outside of the terminal is nothing to write home about. Also, just out of curiosity, can you tell me when this flight was booked?" I was curious to see when they had made the decision to give me das boot, to see if anything I had said in my Captain's Hearing would have actually made a difference.

"Yes, it looks like it was booked on Wednesday, ma'am."

"Wednesday?" *Wednesday!?* A full four days before my hearing? Now I *really* regret not TP-ing the promenade.

"Yes ma'am Wednesday. Will that be all?"

"I guess so."

When I got to the hotel, I was surprised to see that they a.) had heard of me, and b.) handed me a food voucher for the hotel restaurant. RCI must not have communicated that I had been fired and should not be afforded such luxuries. While eating in a sit down restaurant by myself was a sufficiently depressing way to end the night, I felt that a trip to the bar to "drown my troubles" was compulsory after being fired. Yes, a healthy dose of wallowing in my own self-pity would surely make me feel better.

Being at a bar on a Sunday night is disheartening enough, add to it the fact that I was alone and drinking tequila and diet coke with no less than two cherries—a signature drink I have dubbed the "Crass Sombrero"—and my life was just depressing enough to elicit the ear of the bartender.

"Rough day?" he asked.

"Is it that obvious?"

He looked around and upon seeing not a single soul in the bar on a Sunday night he responded in the affirmative. "Nobody's ever ordered tequila and diet coke from me before, it sounds gross."

"Let me tell you a little something about tequila. It makes people feel better, it provides hours of entertainment for whoever is exposed to it, it's a great worker and always on time for its shift and it's been given a bad name for some incomprehensible reason that I still don't get!" Maybe something about the word "gross" had triggered my outburst.

"Next one's on the house," he said sheepishly and slunk away.

I was relieved to find that I wasn't too depressed to appreciate a free drink, but after consuming it I retreated to my hotel room to call it a night. After a short while, I found myself sitting on the double bed of a vacant hotel room with my face buried in my hands, crying.

I immediately recalled the tarot card that Kerry had shown me prior to my firing and how eerily accurate it had been. So accurate that I did a double take to see if there were any spears hanging above my head. No such luck.

Suddenly something snapped me from my thoughts. It was my phone ringing.

"Hey so, umm is your flight landing on time?" Meghan asked.

"Oh my God, Meghan, I forgot to call you! Yea, so change of plans…"

After explaining the situation as best I could, I rescheduled my airport pickup for the following day. She obliged. I quickly called my brother and sister to notify them that my homecoming would be a bit delayed and to not blow my cover. That was at least one thing I could control in my life right now. Or so I thought.

The next day I woke up in spacious bed, with a soft pillow under my head, and most noticeably, a window. Waking up and seeing light was not something I was accustomed to and it reinforced my fear that yesterday was not just a bad dream. I was not looking forward to today. True, I had been counting down the days until the end of my contract while I was on the ship, but this isn't how I had wanted it to end. It was like being dishonorably discharged from the army. I could only imagine the amount of times I would have to explain that I was indeed fired for such a petty offense.

To this day, my brother still seems convinced that there was another reason I was fired. But aside from all of the negative connotations and sympathetic looks I would be afforded for the ensuing months, I really wasn't looking forward to hauling all of my belongings onto multiple planes again. Yesterday I had braced myself for it. Yesterday I was ready to get it over with before the disillusionment had time to sink in—like ripping off a band-aid. But today I'd had a sufficient amount of time to process what was happening and remembered the only communication I would have with my friends on the ship would have to take place in a facebook forum, which they would be able to check maybe on a weekly basis if they had time.

Blocking all of that out for the moment, I gathered my belongings and hopped on the hotel shuttle to the airport. Déjà vu set in when again, I wheeled my large duffel bag up to the counter, complete with a guitar in one hand, a large backpack that just barely qualified as a carry-on on my back, and my bag of filthy laundry tied to the outside of my duffel bag but most characteristically dragging on the ground next to it. This time however, my airline ticket did not succumb to a random cyber attack about which nobody could explain.

"Did you want to maybe put that laundry bag in your checked luggage?" the woman at the counter questioned hoping I would oblige for the sake of the guests on the plane.

"I tried to yesterday they said my luggage was over the 50 lb weight limit."

"Are you sure? Why don't you just try to shove it in there."

After five minutes of struggling to make room for my dirty clothes I finally zipped it up, thinking she would give me the benefit of the doubt if it was overweight.

"Oh yea, 53.4 lbs. You're right, you'll need to pay an extra $50 if you want to check this bag."

Apparently the 3.4 pounds would not be overlooked.

"You know there's going to be the same amount of weight on the plane if I put this in my checked baggage or if I carry it right?"

"Sorry ma'am, there's nothing I can do." Sure, doctors can get a stopped heart beating again but this logic somehow could not be defied. I unpacked my clothes once again and threw my 45 lb bag on the scale to give her.

I had not been sitting at the gate more than five minutes when I heard the warning over the speaker: "Passengers are allowed to take one carry-on bag and a personal bag only. If you have more than this you will need to check it at the gate."

I knew they would give me crap for it, but crap I could take. I could not take paying $100 to get my things home. I decided to play dumb until it was my time to board.

"Ma'am you can't bring that many bags on the plane. You're allowed one carry-on and one personal item," she repeated as if she'd said it a million times before or something.

"Oh. When I asked the woman at the ticket counter she said my guitar didn't count as a bag since it could go in the coat check closet," I lied, but was impressed with how swiftly and believable it came out. Until she called my bluff.

"Who told you that?"

"The woman at the ticket counter…I can't remember her name but I specifically asked and she told me it was fine."

Skeptical, she picked up the phone to try and verify this information. I was mentally preparing to put all of my dirty clothes on my body when she hung up the phone. Nobody had answered.

"Well, nobody was there. I'll let you do it this time, but next flight you need to check this extra bag. I really should be charging you for this." All I heard was, "Blah, blah, blah, you don't have to put on your dirty clothes at the moment." Score one for the good guys!

When the plane landed in D.C., I called Meghan to confirm that my flight was of course delayed—this was Delta after all—and that I would call her when I landed in Hartford for her to come pick me up. After hours of waiting around, they announced that our plane would be boarding shortly. Something about the directive encouraged me to go to the bathroom; no easy task with so many bags might I add. As I went to board, the woman taking tickets engaged me in the same discussion about my excess of bags, almost verbatim, and I apologized and promised I would never do it again before shoving my guitar in the coat closet. What I meant was I *hope* I will never

- 253 -

*have* to do it again. Did I mention all the dirty looks I got from the smell of Caribbean sweat and sand emitting from my laundry bag? They were almost as delightful as having to carry around a bag of dirty laundry all day.

Walking through the luxurious first class section I noticed a man whom I had first recognized from an episode of *The Muppet Show* teaching Fozzie Bear how to do the weather. Most normal people probably know him from his multiple decade-long run as a meteorologist, but he will forever be a *Muppet* guest to me. The NBC shirt he was wearing just confirmed in my mind that it was indeed Willard Scott. Willard Scott was on my plane, I looked like I hadn't slept in days, and I was carrying a bag of hazardous waste. [44]

---

[44] This wasn't the first time I felt foolish in the presence of a celebrity. When I was eight years old, my brother and sister somehow came to the conclusion that it would be best if I, the youngest sibling, walked up to Pete Rose at his restaurant in Florida to ask him if I could shake his hand. Always one to succumb to peer pressure, I walked up to him still filled with youthful idealism and faith in humanity, and asked him in my most polite voice if I could shake his hand. Being a southpaw, I naturally stuck out my left hand to shake when he looked at me. Mr. Rose, perhaps not realizing that I was *fucking eight*, stuck out his right hand to shake. After standing there confused for a solid three seconds, I sheepishly put my left hand down and shook his right hand with mine. What kind of dick can't throw a bone to an 8-year-old girl? I guess the same kind that gets himself banned from the sport of baseball. I know that in India some people wipe their ass with their left hand, but this was America, we had toilet paper and were supposed to be kind to children. And that right there, is why you should never be admitted to the Hall of Fame Pete. I'm pretty sure the Commissioner will see things my way when this little anecdote comes out.

Setting aside my dream of becoming Willard Scott's personal assistant, I glanced at my ticket to find my seat. Naturally, it was in the back of the plane. The second to last row to be exact, eliminating my chance of having an empty seat next to me, as the teenage boy behind me had already laid claim to the entire row. I did however, have the honor of carrying my laundry bag past *almost* every row of passengers. Luckily, the plane was so small that it wasn't physically possible for me to get stuck with the middle seat as I had on the earlier flight, as there were only two seats on my side of the plane. I spent nearly the entire flight writing goodbye letters to friends while listening to Celine Dion's *It's All Coming Back to Me Now* on repeat. For some reason, this hit had become a bit of an anthem on the ship, and it only

---

Then there was the time I was in the Southern District of Israel climbing the ancient fortification of Masada. I was on a Birthright trip and we had spent the previous night (after riding camels no less) sleeping in a nomadic Bedouin tent in the middle of the desert. Showers were not exactly abundant, and water pressure was like flying cars to these people. We were awakened at 4 a.m. in order to summit Masada in time for sunrise. It was nice, but as are all sunrises in my opinion, overrated. What was not overrated was the desert sun, and it encouraged a healthy, or perhaps unhealthy amount of sweat in all of us. So I guess it should not have been a surprise that in the gift shop at the bottom of Masada there was another celebrity sighting. I'll have to admit, I did not expect to see Howie Mandell at a gift shop in the middle of the Israeli desert, but there he was. Though I'm not a huge fan of any game show in which a 3-year-old has the same odds of winning as an educated adult, *Bobby's World* graced our television through many years of my childhood. My penchant for running into celebrities at my worst was uncanny.

felt right that I listen to it for at least 80 straight minutes—a feat that I have not been depressed enough to attempt again thankfully. Somewhere around, "There were nights of endless pleasure, it was more than any laws allowed," our plane had landed in the Nutmeg State. I did not appreciate the irony of the lyric.

"Okay," I thought, "after a much delayed first objective in my mission to surprise my parents, it's time for the second stage."

Call Meghan and have her pick me up from the airport.

"Hmm..." I said out loud with the same fear I'd heard in my mother's voice when dad had asked her where her wedding ring was.

I was pretty sure I hadn't dropped my phone in the sink, but I had also frantically searched the seat pocket in front of me, and the one in front of my neighbor, and all of the seat pockets around me, as well as a 30 foot radius of floor near my seat and it was nowhere to be found. One of the flight attendants was kind enough to let me borrow her phone so I could call mine. I should say, I thought she was being kind, in reality she probably just wanted me off of the plane sooner. This was confirmed when somebody called her phone back from my cell.

"Do you speak Spanish?" she asked me.

"What?" I responded, wondering what that had to do with finding my phone and/or getting me off of her plane.

"Somebody called my phone back from an unknown number, but they're only speaking Spanish."

"Oh…um…yea I speak Spanish," I replied, thinking it would be in some way similar to the Spanish audiotapes I'd listened to.

Grabbing the phone from her I spoke into the mouthpiece.

"Hola! Pienso que tiene mi teléfono." Wow, I thought, where did that come from? Maybe I really had picked up Spanish from those tapes. And then she responded.

I would attempt to type what sounded like a 350 word sentence in 7.4 seconds, but at the time it sounded like the adults speaking in a *Peanuts* cartoon.

"Mas despacio por favor, no hablo Español muy bien," I replied, my confidence in the Spanish language shot to hell.

I couldn't really tell if she used any different words or spoke slower per se, but it did sound louder. So at least my hearing was in tact. After a few more exchanges like this the flight attendant's patience had reached a fever pitch and she slowly reached for her phone.

"I need to go, we need to clean this plane so you have to de-board now." There was the slightest bit of sympathy in her eyes as she slowly removed the phone from my ear while I was trying desperately to decipher the cryptic language that this woman claimed was Spanish. Not enough sympathy to let me figure out where my phone was, but that literally could've taken hours the way the conversation was going. Thankfully, one of the men cleaning the plane was Puerto Rican and actually spoke Spanish.

If I may add a quick side note to all of my Mexican, Argentinean, and Peruvian friends on the ship who never missed an opportunity to compliment my Spanish and tell me how great my accent and vocabulary was: screw you guys. I'm not sure if it's one big joke Spanish speakers have amongst themselves to make gringos believe they can actually speak the language, or if you are all really just that nice, but it has led to several embarrassing and occasionally dangerous situations.

I've even had such self-assurance in my Spanish language skills that I've felt the need to push "2 para Español" on a touch-tone phone when renewing my order of trashy magazines. Of course, I ended up paying for the entire year instead of cancelling which was my original intention, but that's exactly my point. Please stop telling people like myself that we "sound really good" and "are practically fluent" time and time again after we ask if we are actually grasping the language. We are not. Take a lesson from the French here and let us know just how badly we are butchering your language. While the erroneous compliments are appreciated at the time, they will hurt us in the long run.

After I was shoved off of the plane, Andres, a.k.a. my new best friend, followed me to the check-in gate and I explained the situation to him. Most likely motivated by the tears that were clearly about to start flowing out of my eyes like Niagara Falls, Andres sprung to action. He dialed my phone number with his cell and started shouting at the woman in her native tongue. Forty-five seconds later he hung up and informed me that the phone would be sent to Bradley International Airport tomorrow via USPS and I could come pick it up in a few days.

"Wow, thank you so much! What did you tell her? What on God's earth was she saying?"

"She was a cleaning lady at Dulles Airport. She found your phone in a bathroom there and picked it up. I told her that I was a security guard here and she needed to send the phone immediately or I would call her supervisor."

"Well done," I said impressed, and touched that this stranger I had just met was willing to threaten another person's job just to get my $50 flip phone back. Sheepishly, I asked him if I could possibly make a call on his cell phone.

"Last one I promise."

"Sure."

Even more sheepishly I had to ask him how to do it. Phone technology had apparently made some vast improvements while I was at sea. But Andres, ever the gentleman, smiled and asked me what number I wanted. I couldn't remember my friend Meghan's cell phone number but luckily I knew her before cell phones were commonplace and people actually had to remember house numbers. I heard two rings and a woman's voice answered, "The number you have dialed is no longer in service. Please check the number and call again."

This would've been a perfectly timed joke if it were Meghan who said it. Unfortunately, it was not Meghan's voice, and it was instead another annoying speed bump on this trip from

Hell. There goes my plan to surprise my parents. I was just going to have to suck it up and call them. I had known Andres a total of about five minutes, and had inadvertently forced him to leave his job cleaning the plane, yell at a woman he didn't know, ask to borrow his cell phone, and now I was about to break the promise I had made to him not all of ten seconds ago.

"Umm...her phone does not appear to be working at the moment. Would it be possible to make another call?" I asked, trying to avoid promising it would be my last, should this entire Universe continue to align against me and strike down a telephone poll near my house.

"Sure, what number?" he asked, remembering my technological ineptitude.

With the phone up to my ear, I still wasn't exactly sure what I was going to say to my parents.

"Hello?" my mom answered.

"Hey mom!" I tried to sound optimistic.

"Deedee? Where are you? Are you okay?" she asked, aware that I only made phone calls while we were docked in Galveston, Texas, on Sundays.

"Yeah, I'm fine. Uhh I'm actually at Bradley Airport...I'll explain later, can you come pick me up?"

"Yeah we'll be there soon. Whose phone is this?"

"Thanks, see you soon," pretending not to hear her last question.

As I walked through the vacant airport, past all of the various closed *Hudson News* stands and restaurants, I found my way to the also empty, baggage claim. Those of you who have had the pleasure of landing at BDL after 10 p.m. can relate, the other 99% of you can imagine. There was not a single soul left at the baggage claim, and my bright red duffel had gotten caught on something and was slamming up against the ~~medal~~ median, making it look even more pathetic than it already was. I dropped my dirty laundry bag and guitar on the floor as I went to retrieve it, ripped it in the process of trying to un-snag it, and rolled my sorry looking ass to the pickup area.

My parents must've been alarmed to see their youngest daughter in such a condition. They hadn't seen me in months and now here I was, arriving abruptly from a foreign cruise ship and looking like I had jumped overboard and walked the nearly 2,000 miles from Galveston. Immigrants arriving to Ellis Island looked more put together than I did, although I certainly had more belongings in tow.

I got in the car and was greeted with a big, slobbery kiss from my dog. While the Seeing Eye dog foundation Fidelco may not have seen him fit enough to lead the blind, he did possess that indescribable ability that all dogs have to make you feel better. For a minute, I had forgotten about the Captain's Hearing, the fact that I would probably never see my friends again, and the realization that I would soon have to commence another dreaded job search in a very unforgiving economy. That could all wait until tomorrow.

## CHAPTER XVI: THE DAY
## AFTER TOMORROW

*Lesson I've learned the hard way #194: "Go back to school" is the answer to nearly every question I have in life.*

The next morning came all too fast. It felt nice to lie in bed knowing I had no obligations to attend to. No dodge ball tournament to plan, no guests to assist off a ship and back to their real lives, and no balloons to blow up for whichever various celebration was coming up next. That's the sweet part of being fired. The bitter part is the shame, the lack of money flow, and the general and overwhelming feeling of failure. This is also where not having any goals or ambition in life becomes an issue and you're not really sure where to take that next step. That's when my phone rang.

"Hey loserface! I hear you got canned. What are you gonna do next?" It was Grace, one of my best friends and former roommate at Miami University.

"So nice to hear from you Grace. No plans as of yet, I've been back for about nine hours, only one of which I've been awake for, so..."

"Oh my God, you should totally come live with us for the rest of the semester! That would be so fun. Carli isn't taking classes either and Beth broke her foot and skips class all the time. So you would have plenty of company."

"How'd Beth break her foot?"

"She slipped on ice coming out of Stadium at 2 a.m."

"Well that sounds like a sober injury. Umm, what would I *do* all day?"

"I don't know, go to baseball games, day drink, go to the lake? The *fun* part of college without the essays and exams?" She responded, disgusted that I had showed the least bit of concern for my future.

"Obviously I would do it in a heartbeat. I have nothing tying me down here, I just feel like that's not exactly the responsible thing to do."

"Since when are you about doing the responsible thing?" She had a point; responsibility had never been a rule by which I lived my life. Peer pressure; *that* was an idea I was onboard with.

"Touché." I could feel my very twistable arm about to break off. "What should I tell my parents?" After all, they had invested close to $100,000 in my post-secondary education. I felt as if I owed them something more than the ability to label and identify the rivers of Central Asia.

"Tell them you are too distraught to join the real world just yet and need a few more weeks in college to transition yourself. Hey, whatever happened to that book you said you might write about your time on the ship? Did you ever start that? You could tell them you were working on that for six weeks right?"

On a previous check-in phone call to Grace, I believe the first day we docked in Galveston and I was able to make phone calls, I tried to tell her in the short span of about 10 minutes (all I could afford to spend on the phone while in port) about all the crazy stories I was accumulating at sea. I suggested then, as I am sure I did on many other phone calls, that I could write a book based on these shenanigans.

"Grace, you're a genius! That's a great idea. Working on a cruise ship was an even better story than I thought it would be, and at least my getting fired wouldn't be completely in vain. That will certainly make a better conclusion than..."

"Than if you had succeeded?" Grace chimed in.

"Well I'm not sure I would phrase it like that, but..."

"I would. Just kidding...kind of. Who cares!? Just drive down here as soon as you can. I'll go tell Carli she has a new roommate."

# CONCLUSION

After a sublime six weeks of college living sans the classes, I ultimately went on to work at Coppercreek Camp in California as a camp counselor; Keystone, Colorado as a ski instructor; and eventually I ended up applying to Princess Cruises as a youth staffer. I was chasing the high that I had received from my first contract on a ship, because the truth was, I thought about it all the time. My old friends and their office jobs didn't seem as fun, the places I visited daily were a far cry from the French Riviera, and paying for rent really sucks. As badly as I wanted to get off that ship when I was on it, I really missed it. Like, a lot.

After my contract on Princess—and yes, I finished the entire contract without getting fired—I realized that it wasn't so much sailing on the open waters, or the majestic destinations we visited daily, and it certainly was not the money that I missed, but the people. Never before, and never since, have I found myself surrounded by so many fun and diverse people for such a long period of time.

And so, while this book started out as an excuse to enjoy college for another month and a half, it has served as a cathartic release from a bitter circumstance, and at the same time, hopefully enlightened any curious readers as to the goings on of cruise ship life that you can't learn in a guidebook. To anybody considering working on a cruise ship, it is an experience that you will never forget and I would absolutely recommend it.

To anybody about to vacation on a cruise, tip your bartenders and avoid the health center at all costs.

## Acknowledgements

First and foremost, I would like to acknowledge myself, for my ability to actually complete this book with no real deadlines or ambition. I have a newfound respect for authors who can write and publish a book while the same president is in office. Next, I would like to thank my parents, who always reminded me of that very misleading adage, "do what you love and the money follow." Thereby lulling me into a false sense of security from which I will probably never recover. Doing "what I loved" earned me about $3.46 per hour, until my inevitable firing, which led to zero income flow. But in all seriousness, thank you for always encouraging me to follow my dreams, no matter how asinine they may be.

A big shout-out goes to my former college roommates, Beth Brownson, Caroline Furlong, Kristen "Welky Welk" Welker, Grace Andrews, and Carli Calderone; who, after I was fired and unable to face the real world, unanimously chose to harbor me, a shell of a human at the time, and nursed me back to emotional stability with a combination of house parties and day drinking on the deck. Everybody needs friends like these.

Editing accolades go to Mandy Presser, and to a greater extent Grace Andrews, who, despite working for approximately 900% less than the cheapest editor I could find, adhered to the strict deadlines I placed upon her with little regard for her two young children, of whom she was the primary caretaker. This is why I have agreed to sign a copy of her book at a discounted rate, but all of the mistakes in here are totally her fault.

I would like to thank Sydney Morin, who verbally agreed to pay 20% of my legal fees should this book elicit a lawsuit. It's in writing now Sydney. Also J. Maarten Troost, one of my favorite authors who took the time to write back to a novice author trying to navigate her way through the often confusing process of producing a book, your words helped more than you know. Everybody do themselves a favor and pick up a copy of *The Sex Lives of Cannibals*—you won't be disappointed.

Lastly, I would like to thank all of the readers and/or lawyers who made it to the end of this book. I would say if it was able to entertain at least one person it will have been worth it...but I would be lying through my teeth because it's f-ing time consuming to write a book, and then publishing it is an entirely different and tedious process. I digress. Thank you all for reading (and hopefully buying) this book, and I'll be seeing you on the high seas.

*\*\*Disclaimer: All of the names in this book have been changed in order to protect the parties' privacy and the possible humiliation that may result from having to explain some of these stories to their friends and families. All of the preceding stories are based on actual events. In some instances, literary license has been taken.*

# References

[1]Garin, Kristoffer A. *Devils on the Deep Blue Sea*. New York, NY: Penguin Group, 2006.

[3]Vinton, K. (2016). Meet the Richest Billionaires in the Middle East. *Forbes Magazine,* 1 Mar. 2016: http://www.forbes.com/sites/katevinton/20 16/03/01/meet-the-richest-billionaires-in-the-middle-east/#187e0e3927a4.

[6]Febin, A.K. (2007). Evolution of Flags of Convenience. *Shipping Law Notes.* http://shippinglawtimes.blogspot.com/2007 /12/evolution-of-flags-of-convenience.html.

[8]Shaw, J. Flag of Convenience—or Flag of Necessity? *Pacific Maritime Magazine*, Vol 34 (09), 1 Sept. 2016.

[10]McCaffrey, S. *The Law of International Watercourses*. Oxford, England: Oxford International Law Library, 2007.

[11]United Nations Convention on the Law of the Sea (1982). http://www.un.org/depts/los/convention_ag reements/texts/unclos/unclos_e.pdf.

[14]Princess Lines fined in whale's death (2007). http://www.nbcnews.com/id/16879150/ns/ us_news-environment/t/princess-cruise-

lines-fined-whales-death/#.WBjtLJMrLL8, 29 Jan. 2007.

[15]Martinson, J. (1999). Cruise line fined $18m for dumping waste at sea. *The Guardian.* 21 Jul. 1999. https://www.theguardian.com/world/1999/jul/22/janemartinson.

[16]Walker, J. (2011). Fox News Focuses on Dangerous Cruise Ship Medical Care. http://www.cruiselawnews.com/2011/05/articles/passenger-rights/fox-news-focuses-on-dangerous-cruise-ship-medical-care/.

[21]Walker, J. (2010). Update on Death of Royal Caribbean Crew Member Neha Chhikara. http://www.cruiselawnews.com/tags/neha-chhikara/, 28 Mar. 2010.

[23]McCarthy, R. (2006). 1,000 feared dead as ferry sinks in Red Sea. *The Guardian.* *https://www.theguardian.com/world/2006/feb/04/topstories3.egypt.* 3 Feb. 2006.

[24]Langewiesche, W. (2004). A Sea Story. *The Atlantic.* May, 2004.

[25]Sawer, P. Duffin, C. Malnick, E. & Mendick, R. (2012). Costa Concordia: The inside story of the night of Friday, January, 13. *The Telegraph,* 21 Jan. 2012.

[26]Costa Concordia transcript: Coastguard orders captain to return to stricken ship. (2012). *The Guardian.* 17 Jan. 2012.

[27]Cuomo, C. (Reporter). (2012, January 20). Cruise Ship Confidential [Television series episode]. In *20/20*. ABC.

[28]http://www.cruiseshipdeaths.com/Deaths_By_Date.html.

[30]http://www.businessdictionary.com/definition/gross-misconduct.html.